8/24

To Thine
Own Self
Be True

To Thine Own Self Be True

Shakespeare as Therapist and Spiritual Guide

DAVID RICHO

Paulist Press
New York / Mahwah, NJ

Cover image by luceluce/Shutterstock.com
Cover design by Sharyn Banks
Book design by Lynn Else

Library of Congress Cataloging-in-Publication Data
Names: Richo, David, 1940– author.
Title: To thine own self be true : Shakespeare as therapist and spiritual guide / David Richo.
Description: Paperback. | Mahwah, NJ : Paulist Press, 2023. | Summary: "To Thine Own Self Be True presents quotations from Shakespeare's plays that present a delightful and clear portrait of human wholeness"—Provided by publisher.
Identifiers: LCCN 2022044988 (print) | LCCN 2022044989 (ebook) | ISBN 9780809156238 (paperback) | ISBN 9780809187843 (ebook)
Subjects: LCSH: Shakespeare, William, 1564–1616—Quotations. | Human behavior in literature. | Human beings in literature. | Conduct of life in literature. | Spirituality in literature.
Classification: LCC PR2892 .R55 2023 (print) | LCC PR2892 (ebook) | DDC 822.3/3—dc23/eng/20221024
LC record available at https://lccn.loc.gov/2022044988
LC ebook record available at https://lccn.loc.gov/2022044989

ISBN 978-0-8091-5623-8 (paperback)
ISBN 978-0-8091-8784-3 (e-book)

Published by Paulist Press
997 Macarthur Boulevard
Mahwah, New Jersey 07430
www.paulistpress.com

Printed and bound in the
United States of America

For Esme

…be sure
I count myself in nothing else so happy
As in a soul remembering my good friends;
And, as my fortune ripens with thy love,
It shall be still thy true love's recompense:
My heart this covenant makes, my hand thus seals it.

—*Richard II*, Act II, Scene 3

Contents

🜊

Acknowledgments ix

Introduction xi

Part One: Who Are We? 1

1. Love, the Heart Energy of Humanness 3

2. Ego and Humility 14

3. Working through Grief 18

4. Expressing Healthy Anger 28

5. Confronting our Fears 32

6. Our Shadow Side 39

7. The Gift of Joy 46

8. Knowing and Showing Our True Self 51

Part Two: What Happens to Us 57

9. When Things Change 59

CONTENTS

10. The Mystery of Time..64

11. Meaningful Coincidence 69

12. Fate and Chance 73

13. Our Friendly Natural World 80

14. The Spiritual World...85

15. The Journey to Wholeness 90

16. Death..94

Part Three: Spiritual Practices 99

17. Showing and Being Compassion 101

18. A Life of Virtue and Integrity..............................107

19. Sharing Our Gifts 113

20. Restoring Ourselves through Suffering..............117

21. From Revenge to Reconciliation.........................122

22. Making Amends..127

23. Peacemaking within and around Us....................132

24. Gratitude for Graces 136

25. Prayer 140

Epilogue..145

Appendix 147

Acknowledgments

ॐ

I deeply appreciate my teacher, Mark Ferrer. Mark is a luminous ally on the art-path to humanness. In his Shakespeare and poetry classes, he creates a holding environment in which I keep finding the "more" of who I am, a discovery that is always comforting and challenging. But most important is the honor of having him as my lifelong friend.

I also appreciate my editor, Paul McMahon, who believes in my work and has always been a source of friendly encouragement. Paul knows that my writings are my spiritual practice. He joins me in that with great aplomb. Regarding this book, Paul was the first to see its mirthful element, a feature, I hope, of all my books.

> Well, my companion friends,
> If this but answer to my just belief,
> I'll well remember you. (*Pericles*, Act V, Scene 1)

David Richo
Santa Barbara

Introduction

ॐ

Women...
Good sirs, take heart...

—*Antony and Cleopatra*, Act IV, Scene 15

Becoming fully human is a task I have been working at for a while, with no end in sight yet but always with hope at heart. For many years I knew any psychological help should come not only from Psychology 101, Freud, and Jung. Zen masters and mystics help us with cultivating a healthy spirituality. Yet I knew, too, that in this instance, there is another voice to listen to.

I kept looking for someone who might approach the topic of integrating psychology and spirituality from imagination and wisdom rather than only from the science of psychology or spiritual literature. That led me to Shakespeare. He digs deeply into the terrain of the human psyche in inventive, unique, visionary, and compassionate ways. He kindly assists us with comfort and firmly afflicts us with challenge on the potholed path to humanness.

My appeal for Shakespeare goes back to my freshman year of high school, where we read *The Merchant of Venice* and had to memorize Portia's "The quality of mercy" speech—which I notice I can still recite. In the many years since then, I have continued to see, read, study, and contemplate each of the plays. I have gathered, and cherished, many quotations from them. I have been choosing the ones that offer uncanny insights into the human condition and on how to make the most of it, to find wisdom in it, and to grow through, despite its labyrinthine ways.

Gradually, I have come to see that the passages that struck me were not only wise insights, but they also presented a reliable recipe for psychological health and spiritual wholeness. Together the quotations offered a *program*—a set of recommendations—for healthy and upright living. I could see in them just what it takes to build self-esteem, integrity, psychological health, and spiritual maturity. Recently, I found confirmation and help from Harold Bloom's book *Shakespeare: The Invention of the Human*, which shows how Shakespeare basically constructed our human nature as well as our language. Ralph Waldo Emerson noticed this too: "He [Shakespeare] wrote the text of modern life."

In this book, I present the components of humanness as described by Shakespeare. We can find out so much about how to evolve psychologically and spiritually using a frame of quotations from his plays and contemplating their meaning.

I am a Shakespeare buff not a scholar. I am also a psychotherapist with fifty years' experience and the author of numerous self-help and spiritual books. In this book, I write as a psychotherapist and spiritual practitioner with the aid of Shakespeare, consummate spiritual guide and astute commentator on human character. My primary focus here is on how we can find ways to become more fully human with the Bard as our ally and coach. This is certainly quite a knotty project, but Shakespeare will give us generous clues on how to do the untying.

Shakespeare is the original psychologist.

—Harold Bloom, *Shakespeare:
The Invention of the Human*

How Shakespeare Helps Us Be Human

Let's begin with appreciating the wisdom already and always in ourselves, what Shakespeare calls "wholesome wisdom" in *Othello* (Act III, Scene 1). In the Jungian view, the psyche of every one of us contains the entire repository of human wisdom, gathered over the ages. Knowledge of facts requires learning. But somewhere inside us there is already a full treasury of wisdom about life, an entire accurate playbook about how to flourish as stable and healthy human beings. Shakespeare puts this playbook into words that grip and hold us. We are entranced by his language and multileveled discernment. We also realize that what he says resounds in us as familiar. We are not being informed about what we don't know; we are being reconnected to what we always knew, thanks to our legacy from the collective human treasury.

Shakespeare's wisdom is one with our own wisdom and with traditions the world over. We see ourselves more vividly in the family of humanity because of his work and words. As we access the universal truth that has long reposed silently in us like a sleeping giant, we discover ways to deepen our sense of our human story and become better at living it.

Shakespeare also takes us a step further. We go beyond mere understanding of his words or even grasping his insights. We notice that his words touch us *personally*, evoke our feelings, become directly meaningful to our present life circumstances. Realizations can then become self-actualizations, experiences of an empowering truth, and ultimately life changing. Meaning is participatory. It happens *between* humans, in this instance between Shakespeare and us. It is this experiential empowerment that makes the transmission from Shakespeare to us deep, lasting, and significant.

Most of us find Shakespeare complex and difficult to understand because of his antiquated English and poetics. I have found a way to make things easier. In grammar school, we learned to reduce fractions to their "lowest common denominator." I have noticed that same possibility in working with the words of Shakespeare. Not only his thoughts but any complex concept can be restated in simple terms. Deeply meaningful statements can even be reduced to truisms. For instance, this statement from *Macbeth* certainly has depth:

> Give sorrow words. The grief that does not speak
> Whispers the o'erfraught heart and bids it break.
> (Act IV, Scene 3)

We can easily restate it this way: "Let your grief out because if you don't it will become more painful to you later." That is a fact known to everyone, a truism. One needs no Shakespeare to come back from the dead to tell us this. It has become a cliché of the self-help movement. However, the possibility of reduction to simple terms does not mean that the original statement is superficial or trivial. It still has depth.

How does the depth in the words of Shakespeare, or of any wise writer or teacher, reveal itself? There are many ways but three stand out:

> *Experiential*: We feel a match with our own experience; this hits home. Shakespeare is like me.
>
> *Multi-leveled*: We keep discovering new levels of meaning in the words. Shakespeare's insights grow with me in the eras of my life.
>
> *Similar*: We find the same truth in other sources. In this way, we may also go beyond our personal experience and see a universal agreement with Shakespeare. We are touching into the collective unconscious of humanity. Therefore, Shakespeare's wisdom sounds familiar.

Introduction

Each of the three elements have to do with readiness, the time we are moved by words aligns with the time we are ready to take them in:

> *Experiential*: We are in a life situation that makes certain words stand out to us.
>
> *Multi-leveled*: We are of an age and maturity to become aware of deeper levels of meaning than we noticed before.
>
> *Similar*: We keep reading and listening to find similar statements from other sources that confirm and expand on what we see in Shakespeare.

The first happens in an existential moment of heightened experience; the second happens over the years; and the third happens whenever we keep expanding what we read and hear.

Let's look in more detail now at each of the three using the above quotation from *Macbeth* about showing our grief.

Experiential: We may be hurting because we have been keeping our sadness about a loss inside, unexpressed. Now we can name our feeling of grief, share it with someone we trust, and experience the impact of our grief. When we make a connection to our own lives in what we read, we tap into the farther reaches of ourselves and of our life experience. For instance, when I first read *Macbeth* as a senior in high school, I did not even notice these two lines. There was no match between great grief and my experience at age seventeen. There was also no one to whom I could safely show my vulnerability, had I even dared admit I held grief inside me at all. Now, far from high school, I can allow myself to know my own griefs and share them openly with those I can trust. The words of Shakespeare thus become valuable to our health and growth when we take them as wise recommendations or suggestions. In this book we will be finding ways to help that happen.

TO THINE OWN SELF BE TRUE

Multi-leveled: We see—and need to see—the plays of Shakespeare more than once in our lifetime. We see each version of the plays at new levels of absorbability in each era of our lives. At each viewing we hear or notice statements that emphatically resound in us precisely because of the time of life we are in. I have revisited *Macbeth* over the years after my introduction to it in high school. Each time, a different set of statements and situations on the stage jumps out at me. This is an example of synchronicity, meaningful coincidence between the past and the present or between what we need to know, our readiness to know it, and help from a source that describes it. Recall the common adage: "When the student is ready, the teacher appears." The Bard knew this too; Hamlet says, "The readiness is all" (Act V, Scene 2).

Over the years I have saved all the Shakespeare quotations that struck me, even the ones from high school. I have continually noticed new meanings in what had moved me in the past. For instance, once I was drawn to the quotation from *Macbeth* about grief, I kept finding new levels of depth and new forms of help. Gaining help later from something that has struck us before is another marked example of how synchronicity works—we find a meaningful coincidence between what we heard in the past and its later usefulness. An example of this idea is in the story, "The Peasant Marey" by Fyodor Dostoyevsky: "It must have lain hidden in my soul, though I knew nothing of it, and it rose suddenly to my memory when it was needed."

Memory is like an attic. We store something there without a fully identified reason. But later, a need arises, and we know in that instant why we had saved it. We remember lines from great literature, the Bible included, because someday we will need them to make it through a chill or frenzied night. Here too, our readiness is what matters.

Similarity: We make associations in our mind between a truth we have grasped and similar truths from other sources. For instance, regarding the lines about grief in *Macbeth*, here is the same idea from the Turkish poet Nazim Hikmet in "On Living":

> You must grieve for this right now
> —you have to feel this sorrow now—
> for the world must be loved this much
> if you're going to say "I lived." (translated by Randy
>   Blasing and Mutlu Konuk Blasing)

I also see a spin-off of Shakespeare's idea in *The Little Prince*: "It's such a secret place, the land of tears."

Another example is from John Donne in his poem, "Elegy on Mistress Boulstred":

> Grief wears and lessens, that tears breath affords.

The modern poet Eavan Boland, in "Pomegranate," takes us a step further:

> If I defer the grief, I will diminish the gift.

The similarity in a variety of literary traditions is indeed meaningful coincidence, synchronicity. Likewise, in this instance, as above, our readiness makes the difference. We see similarities exactly and only when we are ready to "get the message"—another form of meaningful coincidence.

How to Use This Book

I have chosen twenty-five components of and challenges to humanness, each presented in a chapter. Each chapter begins with a short introduction to the topic as it is described generally in psychology or spirituality. Then I present quotations from

Shakespeare's plays based on that theme. Each is meant to be pondered. After each Shakespeare quotation I offer a short re-phrase in modern English. For some quotations I do more than translate into modern English. I let my own thoughts rise out of the associations the quotation has kindled. I encourage you to do the same. We can use the quotations as springboards into our own inner wisdom, the gift that comes from our pondering. At the end of each chapter and subsection, I present a personal reflection. This is my own take on the points made in the quotations and includes my own expanding of the topic. I recommend that you also record your understanding of the topic in your journal. Then we shall have three authors of this book: Shakespeare, me, and you. What an honored—and fun—collaboration!

Every passage that I have selected from Shakespeare takes us further into who we are and can be, both psychologically and spiritually. The quotations are wonderfully imaginative spring-boards and present a rich medley of Shakespeare's insights into human nature, what happens to and within us humans, and how we can grow from our experience. Thus, the book is divided into those three areas:

In part 1, we explore who we are; in part 2, we look at what happens to us in life; and in part 3, we present specific psycho-logical and spiritual suggestions from Shakespeare about how to put our themes into practice so that we can expand and express our wonderful potential for wholeness, already and always within us.

Our use of the word *wholeness* reminds us to consider the word *self* in the title of this book, a quotation from Act I, Scene 3 of *Hamlet*. The word is used in this book in two ways: it refers both to our personal identity and to our larger cosmic life. We are true to our own personal self when we live with integrity, fulfill our potential, and relate to others effectively. We are true to our higher—cosmic—Self, to our God within, to our Buddha nature, when we act with unconditional loving-kindness and dedicate ourselves to our evolutionary purpose to co-create a world of justice, peace, and love. Our personal self is unique; our higher Self is the same in all of us. Our self develops from psychological work; our higher Self, always already fully developed, emerges even more as our spiritual practices take effect. In the quotations that follow we will find in Shakespeare the insights and practices that can help us fulfill both identities, ultimately only one. Integrating them is our aim in this book—with the Bard's expert help.

Journaling

As stated above, I recommend journal writing as a way of working with the topic of each chapter and any of the quotations. This will enrich your experience of Shakespeare's wisdom and may awaken your own wisdom about what you are reading. In your journal, describe the relevance of the content of the chapter or Shakespeare quotations to your present or past issues and challenges. Then consider how to apply the content and your reflections to your daily life, especially in terms of growth toward spiritually conscious, healthy, and aware humanness. Find comfort in what you are exploring and open to gratitude for the grace of finding out so much about yourself.

Look back at your journal after a few months and notice if any of the quotations have taken on new levels of meaning. Add quotations from other sources that strike you. I have found that this practice has deepened my sense of the meaning of life, and, even more intriguing, my purpose on the planet. I am hoping this happens for you as you work with what follows.

Consider the following example of how contemplating a topic can help us grow psychologically and spiritually. A central teaching in Buddhism is the inescapability of impermanence. We see the same theme in Shakespeare's Sonnet 15:

TO THINE OWN SELF BE TRUE

Everything that grows
Holds in perfection but a little moment.

We can state this simply: "Yes, everything is transitory." However, we may not yet have fully embraced this truth in our personal experience. We may believe it intellectually but not be practicing it in daily life. For instance, we may cling to our partner with full trust that our relationship will last a lifetime. When our partner leaves us for a new relationship, we are shocked, devastated, and thrown for a loop. Then we realize that we never really believed in impermanence in a fully assenting way. For instance, we never imagined it would apply to *our* relationship. The depth of any spiritual teaching is in how far within us we take it, how fully we let ourselves experience it, how definitely we have grasped that there is no exemption from it. Then meaning as *informative* becomes meaning as *impactful*. This is also how we recognize levels of depth in what we read or experience and deepen ourselves as well. We too contain innumerable levels of depth; one lifetime is insufficient to plumb them all. (Of course, it is likewise true that no one can fully plumb all of Shakespeare.)

Finally, I share some comments on my choices of quotations and how I line them up. All of Shakespeare plays are represented in this book but not in the order in which they are written. They are arranged by topic. The lineup of quotations in each individual chapter is organized to develop a topic so that it keeps building our understanding of it. My listings do not therefore necessarily follow the order of quotations in a particular play. Thus, a quotation from Act III that introduces a topic may follow a quotation from Act II that deepens its meaning.

I present the lines in the plays without referring to the context in which they appear or the characters who say them. I am not presenting a literary treatment of Shakespeare's plays. This is my attempt at writing a self-help book with extensive assistance from the Bard. We therefore attend to *content* not context.

Introduction

Here are examples of how the context of a quotation might be a distraction from our self-help purpose: Othello says to Iago, "If thou dost love me, / Show me thy thought." In the play, Othello says this with great angst. He is longing for information that he believes Iago is withholding. Indeed, Iago only wants to tease and torment him. In this book we concentrate not on the cruelty of Iago, the literary context, but on how sincere love between people includes trust and sharing: when people really love us, they share their inmost thoughts and feelings with us. We can certainly hear this truth in the two lines that are quoted.

Here is one more example of attention to word rather than context: In *Richard III*, Buckingham may not be sincere when he says, "Now cheer each other in each other's love." But our interest is in how joy is part of mutual love, so we focus on that element clear from the literal words.

I have not included familiar epigrams such as "Brevity is the soul of wit." My choice of quotations is based on the criterion of in-depth comments on the human condition. My interest is in what Shakespeare said that helps us to know ourselves, to contact the inmost regions in our psyche, to show love to ourselves and others, and to guide us toward a worthwhile life. Epigrams are quips, too facile to serve those lofty purposes.

Part One

Who
Are We?

1

Love, the Heart Energy of Humanness

L ove can be described with three tender Cs: a caring, committed connection. Such a rich expression of love begins with oneself and expands to include others. We love ourselves when we keep our body healthy and our mind open. We love ourselves when we are committed to acting with loving-kindness and to showing integrity in all our actions. Love thus naturally combines physical, psychological, and spiritual health.

Our need for love from others is balanced by our need to show love to them, whether they love us or not. No matter how people treat us or what happens to us, we can go on loving. Our capacity to love is limitless and never goes away. An evolutionary drive in us wants what all nature wants, more consciousness, more cooperation, and more connectedness. Nature wants us to co-create with her a world of caring, committed connection. This is what love is and can be.

Love is a depth experience. Depth means that there is *more* going on than what appears on the surface. We see more than someone's face or body; we see more than a planet; we see a heart. Love empowers us and shares its power with others. Love is transcendent; it reaches out to more than our near and dear. It expands until it becomes universal and unconditional.

Let's now explore some themes of love and its phases in Shakespeare's plays.

In High Romance

Reason and love keep little company. (*A Midsummer Night's Dream*, Act III, Scene 1)

In high romance love is blind. We act on emotion or compulsion rather than on reason.

Kindness in women, not their beauteous looks,
Shall win my love. (*The Taming of the Shrew*, Act IV, Scene 2)

It is loving kindness rather than physical beauty that attracts me and leads me to love you.

Even such a passion doth embrace my bosom:
My heart beats thicker than a feverous pulse;
And all my powers do their bestowing lose,
Like vassalage at unawares encountering
The eye of majesty. (*Troilus and Cressida*, Act III, Scene 2)

All my mental powers are absorbed in one focus, passionate love, and I am its servant. (The next quotation shows the other side of this.)

But love, first learned in a lady's eyes,
Lives not alone immured in the brain;

Love, the Heart Energy of Humanness

But, with the motion of all elements,
Courses as swift as thought in every power,
And gives to every power a double power,
Above their functions and their offices.
It adds a precious seeing to the eye;
A lover's eyes will gaze an eagle blind;
A lover's ear will hear the lowest sound…
And when Love speaks, the voice of all the gods
Makes heaven drowsy with the harmony. (*Love's Labor Lost*,
    Act IV, Scene 3)

Love endows our mind and senses so they can transcend ordinary thought and behavior and thus increase their powers.

Yet, wooing thee, I found thee of more value
Than stamps in gold or sums in sealed bags;
And 'tis the very riches of thyself
That now I aim at. (*The Merry Wives of Windsor*, Act III,
    Scene 4)

As I continued to court you, I found great value in you as a person and that discovery showed me what I am really seeking.

— ☪ —

When we are overcome by adrenaline and dopamine, our cerebral cortex, the reasoning component of our brain, goes offline. It is, therefore, best not to make big decisions about a relationship when the flames of romance are in full flourish. In *Paradise Lost*, John Milton gives similar wise advice:

Take heed lest passion sway
Thy judgment to do aught, which else free will
Would not admit. (*Paradise Lost*, Bk. VIII)

WHO ARE WE?

We can enjoy the experience of romantic passion but not make a full commitment to a relationship until the flames die down and the smoke clears. Our model is Ulysses, who enjoyed the sirens' song while remaining safe from closeness to them—which would have been a self-destructive choice.

Many of us make the mistake of equating physical beauty with goodness, a common feature of romantic attachment. We imagine that, if someone is attractive, he or she has no dark side, can be trusted unconditionally, and will always match actions with looks. As we mature, we realize that goodness shown in daily choices, and that actions is what matters. Likewise, we no longer believe that if someone is beautiful, we will automatically be happy with him or her. As we grow in wisdom, we let go of superstitions like this. We trust someone based on ongoing evidence of trustworthiness that is shown in daily consistent behavior. Then we may notice a change in our criteria for a partner. As mature adults, it is not arm candy but unarmed openness that we cherish.

We know a relationship is real and healthy when the presence of the other engenders an oxytocin response in us. Oxytocin is the hormone that gives us a warm comforting feeling and a sense of security. We distinguish that from an attachment that simply feels warm and fuzzy, a dopamine response. That is not a secure basis for connection and commitment in an intimate relationship.

We also need to see that the one we "love" is up for working things out with us when problems arise. We need to see that the one we are so happy to be with offers a caring, committed connection. Otherwise, night may be falling when it looks to our awestruck sight that day is dawning.

The Meaning, Pain, and Power of Love

With love's light wings did I o'er–perch these walls.
For stony limits cannot hold love out
And what love can do that dares love attempt. (*Romeo and Juliet*,
   Act II, Scene 2)

*My love is so strong that I can surmount any barriers. No one can
hold back love. Whatever love can do it will dare to do it.*

Look thou but sweet,
And I am proof against their enmity. (*Romeo and Juliet*, Act II,
   Scene 2)

One kindly look from someone who loves me feels like protection.

The sight of lovers feedeth those in love. (*As You Like It*, Act III,
   Scene 4)

Seeing people in love also nourishes those who love.

They do not love that do not show their love. (*Two Gentlemen of
   Verona*, Act I, Scene 2)

Our love is only real when we show it in loving actions.

...who could refrain,
That had a heart to love, and in that heart
Courage to make his love known? (*Macbeth*, Act II, Scene 3)

WHO ARE WE?

We don't hold back when we love and are courageous enough to let our love be known.

Your gentleness shall force
More than your force move us to gentleness. (*As You Like It*, Act II, Scene 7)

Love has more power than coercion.

It is not night when I do see your face. (*A Midsummer Night's Dream*, Act II, Scene 1)

Your radiance illumines the darkness.

The love that follows us sometime is our trouble,
Which still we thank as love. (*Macbeth*, Act I, Scene 6)

We can appreciate a chore that is done out of love.

Then shall you know the wounds invisible
That love's keen arrows make. (*As You Like It*, Act III, Scene 5)

Love itself can be a portal into grief since lovers inevitably hurt one another.

The course of true love never did run smooth. (*A Midsummer Night's Dream*, Act I, Scene 1)

It is a given that conflicts arise in any intimate relationship.

Our separation so abides, and flies,
That thou, residing here, goest yet with me,
And I, hence fleeting, here remain with thee. (*Antony and Cleopatra*, Act I, Scene 3)

True partners/friends are together even when apart. Antony is leaving Cleopatra in Egypt temporarily as he sets out for Rome. He combines apparent opposites: "abides/flies." This reconciles them: "residing/goest," and "fleeting/remain." In a bottomless bond, there is no between only connection, no distance only nearness.

— ॐ —

A gentle approach toward someone has more power than pushing to have him or her soften toward us. However, our gentle approach to others is not meant to be a strategy to get them to act kindly toward us. We act in kindly ways because that has become our style, the standard of relating that we follow.

Love makes us courageous, that is, heart-led, as happened to Romeo. We also see examples of this in familiar stories. For instance, in *The Wizard of Oz* the lion is cowardly, but he nonetheless bravely joins the fight against the witch in order to save Dorothy *because he loves her.* When a theme is common in stories and in our own life experience, it represents an archetype, a common motif in human behavior, a human capacity. Thus, the instinct to be brave when we love is an energy, an inclination in all of us. We can rely on the fact that we have within us what we see on stage.

Love also includes painful times because in any relationship we meet up with the shadow side of ourselves and our partner. The ideal partner we appeared to be and believed our partner was begins to fade and our ego kicks in. Along these lines, St. Augustine wrote quite candidly in his *Confessions*, "What I needed most was to love and to be loved. I rushed headlong into love, eager to be caught. Happily I wrapped those painful bonds around me; and sure enough, I wound up being lashed with the red-hot pokers of jealousy, by suspicions and fear, by bursts of anger and quarrels." Somehow all he says is familiar as we look at the history of our own relationships.

Equality in Love

We came into the world like brother and brother,
And now let's go hand in hand, not one before another. (*The
Comedy of Errors*, Act V, Scene 1)

We are born as equals and we go forward arm in arm.

But love…
Lives not alone immured in the brain;
But, with the motion of all elements,
Courses as swift as thought in every power,
And gives to every power a double power,
Above their functions and their offices. (*Love's Labor Lost*, Act
IV, Scene 3)

*Love is not simply in our minds; it moves through us as quickly as
thought, affecting all we do so that every power in us becomes stronger
and goes beyond itself.*

Such men as he be never at heart's ease
Whiles they behold a greater than themselves,
And therefore are they very dangerous. (*Julius Caesar*, Act I,
Scene 2)

*Some people insist on being on top and their envy is dangerous to
the rest of us.*

Why should their liberty than ours be more? (*The Comedy of
Errors*, Act II, Scene 1)

We all deserve equal freedom.

Let me be that I am and seek not to alter me. (*Much Ado about Nothing*, Act I, Scene 3)

Accept me as I am without trying to change me.

— ۿ —

Love is co-presence. We hold one another in an egalitarian not a hierarchical way. This means that neither one of us is trying to control the other. One of us is not a parent to or master of the other. We are together in equal companionship. We respect one another's differences and appreciate how we complement each other. Our style and goal are respectful mutuality and willing collaboration.

In a healthy relationship, both partners have equal power, regardless of roles, levels of intelligence, or financial status. Power in human relationship is the right and ability to make choices that reflect our own deepest needs, values, and wishes. When power is shared equally, we are not caught in roles of domination and submission. Instead, power is shared and honored equally. Decisions are then made equilaterally. A meeting of minds is the goal of healthy relating not how one person is right or in control. It is such control that poisons love and makes relationships a hell on earth, both for the one wielding the whip and the one at the mercy of it. All this reminds us that it takes a high level of personal psychological and spiritual health to love effectively. This is the challenge that Shakespeare is helping us face.

Love Is Sacred and Universal

Love is holy. (*All's Well that Ends Well*, Act IV, Scene 2)

All love is sacred. Love has a spiritual dimension. (The root of the word *holy* is related to wholesomeness and wholeness.)

Love all, trust a few,
Do wrong to none: be able for thine enemy
Rather in power than use; and keep thy friend
Under thy own life's key: be checked for silence,
But never taxed for speech. (*All's Well that Ends Well*,
    Act I, Scene 1)

Show love to all but trust only the few who deserve it. Be strong in the face of a foe but don't abuse your power. Cherish your friends. Be called to account for being silent but not so talkative that others are burdened.

My bounty is as boundless as the sea,
My love as deep! The more I give to thee
The more I have! The both are infinite. (*Romeo and Juliet*,
    Act II, Scene 2)

Now that I love you, I have more to give than I ever had before, and the more I give to you the more I have in and for myself. This is the prized paradox of authentic love.

Time, force, and death,
Do to this body what extremes you can;
But the strong base and building of my love
Is as the very center of the earth,
Drawing all things to it. (*Troilus and Cressida*, Act IV, Scene 2)

Love, the Heart Energy of Humanness

No matter what happens to us in the ruins of time, in the face of aggression, or even in death, our indestructible love survives. It is a gravity ever keeping us, and everything, firmly connected.

— ༄ —

In true love, we notice qualities of wholeness, wholesomeness, and holiness. Holiness refers to the sacred, something set aside for special reverence. When a relationship has a spiritual foundation, we show each other the honor and reverent attentiveness that we offer to sacred things. In religious practices, we adore the divine. In relationships, we see the divine in one another. In other words, we cherish one another in an unconditionally loving embrace. Our home together is a sacred space. Our actions are meant to reflect our divine nature. This level of spiritual consciousness is rarely mentioned in spiritual books about relationships, but Shakespeare reminds us of it.

Once we see with love, we see truly. If we hold resentment and aggression in our hearts, we do not see who someone really is. It is love that clears the way to a direct perception of other humans—and of ourselves. This follows since love is what we truly are in the depths of our being. Just as we say that God is love, so we can say that we are too, since we are made in the image of divinity. Likewise, since we are here to show love, the two combine in a mature spirituality: we see only with love, and we show only love. In other words, the spiritual path turns out to be acting in accord with our true nature and that of others. Thus, love is not an alien practice; it is acting in solidarity with who each of us is, a holy enterprise indeed.

2

Ego and Humility

Our healthy ego serves as our executive function, what helps us set goals, assess our skills, and then use our interior and exterior resources to fulfill our life purposes. Our inflated ego, however, imagines itself entitled to have what we want whether we put in the uphill effort required to attain it or not.

We might also think that we deserve special treatment, that the world revolves around us, and that we are meant to be in control of what happens. Yet, the powers of the arrogant ego are more limited than we imagine. Indeed, they are really a house of cards without a foundation. In the world of ego, the great pretender, we think we know it all but, in reality, are ignorant of what life is about: intelligent discernment, equality with others, and an effective connection to those we love. All this leads not to chilling arrogance but to a refreshing humility about ourselves. We only truly care about ourselves, take care of ourselves, when we give up ego-selfishness in favor of self-caring and self-giving.

Ego and Humility

The abuse of greatness is, when it disjoins
Remorse from power. (*Julius Caesar*, Act II, Scene 1)

*The worst abuse of greatness comes when those in power disavow
conscience and personal responsibility.*

Bondage is hoarse and may not speak aloud. (*Romeo and Juliet*,
    Act II, Scene 2)

*People subjugated in bondage lose the power to cry out about their
plight.*

O, it is excellent
To have a giant's strength; but it is tyrannous
To use it like a giant. (*Measure for Measure*, Act II, Scene 2)

*It is wonderful to have power, but it becomes despotic when we use
it to dominate others.*

Can honor set a leg? No, or an arm? No, or take away the grief of
    a wound? No. Honor hath no skill in surgery then? No. What
    is honor? A word. What is that word, honor? Air. (*Henry IV,
    Part One*, Act V, Scene 1)

*When we fight to preserve "honor," we do so in order to maintain
ego supremacy or engaging in illusion.*

But man, proud man,
Drest in a little brief authority,
Most ignorant of what he's most assur'd;
His glassy essence, like an angry ape,
Plays such fantastic tricks before high heaven,
As make the angels weep. (*Measure for Measure*, Act II, Scene 2)

WHO ARE WE?

When a person has a distorted sense of his own power, arrogantly denying it's limitations, his fragile authority injures others cruelly. This makes the angels weep as they witness the pain he inflicts.

Uneasy lies the head that wears a crown. (*Henry IV, Part Two*, Act III, Scene 1)

When someone has power, he feels threatened that he might lose it.

Nor I nor any man that but man is
With nothing shall be pleased, till he be eased
With being nothing. (*Richard II*, Act V, Scene 5)

Letting go of our ego is a path to happiness. We are released from stress when we give up our claims to superiority and accept our humble state.

Self-love is not so vile a sin as self-neglecting. (*Henry V*, Act II, Scene 3)

Being selfish is not as bad as not taking care of yourself appropriately.

— ﷽ —

When we grow in integrity, we do not use power over others only for others. We see any power we have as an invitation to serve rather than to dominate. Love and power have come together in our hearts. In other words, integrity and loving-kindness are ultimately one spiritual practice.

A feature of love is compassion for those who suffer, especially because of the pain inflicted by injustice. We not only care about the plight of others; we also desire (aim) to assist them. We not only act justly, we are committed to right the wrong that created the injustice that led to their suffering.

16

When we have power and relate with love, justice does not take the form of retribution. We want to restore to the human community the one who has hurt us or done society wrong. Our sense of justice is not founded on demand for punishment. It is about seeking reconciliation while also asking for amends.

When we are in a position of authority, we want to use it for the good of the group not for our own ends. We see power as an opportunity to serve a greater good. We know power corrupts, so we keep tabs on ourselves and ask for feedback from others on how we are handling the gavel.

Power is the ability to make choices, to act, and to produce an effect. Control is used to maintain order. It becomes negative when it leads us to micromanage, to interfere in the behavior of others, and to make others do what I want them to do.

Here is the difference between true healthy use of power *for* others and control *over* others:

POWER	CONTROL
Leading	Forcing
Power *for* reaching a common goal	Power *over* others
I engage with...	I demand that...
My ego bows to collaboration	My ego is at the helm
Collegial: Egalitarian (shared power)	Unilateral: Authoritarian (abuse of power)
Respectful of others' freedom	Aggressive toward others
Relaxed grasp	Tight grip
Skillful	Unskillful

3

Working through Grief

Grief is how we process impermanence. This entails a radical acceptance of changes and endings, the givens in any life. The experience of grief consists of three main feelings: sadness, anger, and fear: we are sad that something has ended; we are angry that it has been taken away; and we are afraid that it will never be replaced or that our life will be empty without it. As we let ourselves experience these feelings whenever they arise, we move toward a gradual release from the searing pain, the trauma of our loss. The resolving of our grief is the prelude to going on, to continuing our life journey. Our motto can be: "Don't flee or fix, just feel, let go, and move on."

Shakespeare is sympathetic to our human story with all its endings too soon and losses too many. All of us share the human condition. Psychologically, we grieve its craters and canyons. Spiritually, we are called to an engaged compassion for our companions who, like us, suffer so poignantly in this weary world of dissolutions.

— ॐ —

Working through Grief

O grief and time
Fearful consumers, you
Will all devour. (*The Two Noble Kinsmen*, Act I, Scene 1)

Ultimately, endings and the passing of time take charge of our lives.

The origin and commencement of…grief
Sprung from neglected love. (*Hamlet*, Act III, Scene 1)

All our griefs are ultimately about lost love.

My grief lies all within;
And these external manners of laments
Are merely shadows to the unseen grief
That swells with silence in the tortured soul.
There lies the substance. (*Richard II*, Act IV, Scene 1)

My grief is deep inside me, and these ways of showing my lament fail to match how much sadness lies within me.

Each substance of a grief hath twenty shadows,
Which shows like grief itself, but is not so;
For sorrow's eye, glazed with blinding tears,
Divides one thing entire to many objects;
Like perspectives, which rightly gazed upon
Show nothing but confusion, eyed awry
Distinguish form… (*Richard II*, Act II, Scene 2)

Each grief is accompanied by twenty imaginary ones. When sorrow is blinded by tears it makes one thing look like many things. This experience is like perspective in a painting that makes its subject confusing until we see it at a proper angle.

Grief boundeth where it falls,
Not with the empty hollowness, but weight:

19

WHO ARE WE?

I take my leave before I have begun,
For sorrow ends not when it seemeth done. (*Richard II*, Act I,
    Scene 2)

Grief bounces back again when it seems to be over. It keeps feeling heavy. When I made my farewells, I still had more grief to express.

— ༄ —

In the quotations above, we see four characteristics of mourning a loss:

* The loss obsesses us, that is, occupies our conscious thoughts no matter how we try to dismiss it.
* Every ending of a relationship breaks a connection that was important to us, even crucial to our survival. That connection is love—what we feel diminishing when a loss occurs.
* Grief is deeply personal. We feel it in a way that is unique. Other people may try to help us or insist that we "get over it," but they can never really know our unique way of holding our grief—or its mysterious timing.
* It may seem that grief has passed, but it has a way of coming back, we don't know why, nor can we engineer its departure. In that sense, grief is bigger than our minds or bodies, bigger than any technique meant to snuff it out. All we can do is allow it.

We can compare Shakespeare's "O grief [regarding death] and *time*, Fearful consumers..." to this verse in the *Baghavad Gita*: "I am become death, the destroyer [consumer] of worlds" (*BG* 11:32). The word for death, *kala*, also means time. Incidentally, Robert Oppenheimer quoted this passage when the atomic bomb was dropped on Japan in 1945.

Avoiding Our Grief

Hope of revenge shall hide our inward woe. (*Troilus and Cressida*, Act V, Scene 10)

Think therefore on revenge and cease to weep. (*Henry VI, Part Two*, Act IV, Scene 4)

Be comforted:
Let's make us medicines of our great revenge,
To cure this deadly grief. (*Macbeth*, Act IV, Scene 3)

Be this the whetstone of your sword: let grief
Convert to anger; blunt not the heart, enrage it. (*Macbeth*, Act IV, Scene 3)

The four passages above make the same statement: taking revenge and showing rage save us from having to feel grief.

He hath left part of his grief with me,
To suffer with him. (*Othello*, Act III, Scene 3)

He is sad, and by telling me about it, I wind up feeling grief too, his not mine. Meanwhile he avoids experiencing the full thud of his own grief.

You do surely bar the door upon your own liberty if you deny
your griefs to your friend. (*Hamlet*, Act III, Scene 2)

You lose your full freedom when you hide your feelings of grief from those you can trust.

Getting even after being treated unjustly is a primitive but common way of avoiding our grief. We have all heard that "revenge is sweet." Here is the actual quotation from John Milton indicating that it is not so simple:

Revenge, at first though sweet,
Bitter ere long back on itself recoils.

Another way of avoiding the full weight of our own grief is to shift some of it onto others. We tell others of our distresses and thereby decant some of our pain into the vessel of someone else's psyche. Likewise, others might try to do this to us. As we learn the art of maintaining our boundaries, we do not engage in off-loading our distress onto others. Similarly, we do not allow such off-loading by others onto us. We can kindly listen but protect ourselves from carrying the grief of others. We can also recommend therapy, the appropriate venue for the processing of events and consequent feelings.

While sharing our feelings and story with friends can help us to connect with others, we can also lose our connection with others when we hide our grief. It is wiser to share while not off-loading. We then remain free to tell our story and open our hearts but also hold our feelings appropriately.

Comfort in Our Sadness

The venom of such looks we fairly hope
Have lost their quality, and that this day
Shall change all griefs and quarrels into love. (*Henry V*, Act V,
    Scene 2)

We hope they let go of any desire to hurt us and that letting go makes enmity change into amity.

Working through Grief

When we our betters see bearing our woes,
We scarcely think our miseries our foes.
Who alone suffers suffers most in the mind,
Leaving free things and happy shows behind:
But then the mind much sufferance doth o'er skip,
When grief hath mates, and bearing fellowship. (*King Lear*, Act
  III, Scene 6)

*When we see that those whom we admire have the same problems as
us, our own pain eases. The person who is alone in his or her suffering
is the one who suffers most. When others are with us in our grief, our
troubles are more tolerable.*

I do desire thee, even from a heart
As full of sorrows as the sea of sands,
To bear me company and go with me. (*Two Gentlemen of Verona*,
  Act IV, Scene 3)

*I want you with me no matter how sad you are; I still want you to
keep me company.*

Tell them that, to ease them of their griefs,
Their fears of hostile strokes, their aches, losses,
Their pangs of love, with other incident throes
That nature's fragile vessel doth sustain
In life's uncertain voyage, I will some kindness do them. (*Timon
  of Athens*, Act V, Scene 1)

*Let those who suffer know that I am with them in loving-kindness no
matter how heavy their woes.*

Praising what is lost
Makes the remembrance dear. (*All's Well That Ends Well*, Act V,
  Scene 3)

WHO ARE WE?

When we look for the good in what is gone, we cherish it even more.

...for it so falls out
That what we have we prize not to the worth
Whiles we enjoy it, but being lacked and lost,
Why, then we rack the value, then we find
The virtue that possession would not show us
Whiles it was ours. (*Much Ado about Nothing*, Act IV, Scene 1)

We fail to appreciate the value of something while we have it, only when we lose it.

Things without all remedy
Should be without regard: what's done is done. (*Macbeth*, Act III,
    Scene 2)

We do well to accept what we cannot change or fix.

The weight of this sad time we must obey,
Speak what we feel, not what we ought to say. (*King Lear*, Act V,
    Scene 3)

We need to speak the truth about the sadness we see around us and not simply repeat platitudes.

Grief fills up the room of my absent child,
Lies in his bed, walks up and down with me.
Puts on his pretty looks, repeats his words.
Remembers me of all his gracious parts.
Stuffs out his vacant garments with his form.
Then have I reason to be fond of grief. (*King John*, Act III,
    Scene 4)

Working through Grief

My grief for my loss is not so bad when I let myself remember the good times. My inner images and memories of the one I lost keep the person alive in me.

...all these woes shall serve
For sweet discourses in our time to come. (*Romeo and Juliet*, Act
    III, Scene 5)

Someday these painful experiences will be remembered with sweetness and comfort. This same idea is found in the *Aeneid* by Virgil: "*Forsitan et haec meminisse uvabit*" (Perhaps it will [someday] help to remember even these things) (1.203).

Come, and take choice of all my library
And so beguile thy sorrow. (*Titus Andronicus*, Act IV, Scene 1)

Reading is comforting in our times of grief. Self-help and spiritual books are good sources of comfort today.

$$-\;\text{علم}\;-$$

There are valuable and effective ways to find solace in our mourning:

- We act with love no matter how others have acted toward us.
- We share our feelings in fellowship with others, especially those who have experienced similar losses.
- We ask those we trust to accompany us on our path.
- We contact the good in what or whom we have lost.
- We express our authentic feelings rather than being tied to the social conventions that may suppress them.
- We keep those who are gone present in our hearts.

25

- We find comfort in conversations, books, or our own journal.
- We trust that our pain will turn to resolution in the future. We recall the words of Fr. Zossima, in Fyodor Dostoyevsky's *The Brothers Karamazov*: "It's the great mystery of human life that old grief passes gradually into quiet tender joy."

Bringing our Grief to Mother Nature

This shadowy desert, unfrequented woods,
I better brook than flourishing peopled towns:
Here can I sit alone, unseen of any,
And to the nightingale's complaining notes
Tune my distresses and record my woes. (*Two Gentlemen of Verona*, Act V, Scene 4)

In my solitude here in nature, I am happier than I ever have been in town. And the nightingale's song attunes to my own feelings.

Therefore I tell my sorrows to the stones;
Who, though they cannot answer my distress,
Yet in some sort they are better than the tribunes,
For that they will not intercept my tale:
When I do weep, they humbly at my feet
Receive my tears and seem to weep with me;
And, were they but attired in grave weeds,
Rome could afford no tribune like to these. (*Titus Andronicus*, Act III, Scene 1)

26

Working through Grief

I share my sad story with the natural world that listens without interruption, a quality I do not find so easily in people.

— ☾ —

Our grief is meant to pass through us like lightning through a lightning rod. It then goes into, ends up in, the earth. It is Mother Nature who thus finally accepts and grounds our pain. We are physically stabilized by walking on the earth; we are psychologically and spiritually stabilized by giving our feelings to the earth. Our practice of bringing our feelings to nature can happen by walking, by sitting, by dancing in a natural setting, or by any meditative time in nature. Our feelings are natural. When we experience them outdoors or indoors looking out, we are placing them where they belong. We will feel a sense of being held in the arms of Mother Nature. In his poem, "Correspondences," Charles Baudelaire states this profoundly: "Nature is a temple….Man passes there through forests of symbols / Which look at him with understanding eyes." Thus, we feel accompanied by trees, birds, stars, and all the wonderful allies in and of the natural world. In other words, we feel at home. This happens because what is in nature is in us and both are one. Origen, a third-century theologian, adds aptly, "You have within yourself the herds of cattle, flocks of sheep, and the fowls of the air. You are a world in miniature with a sun, a moon, and many stars."

4

Expressing
Healthy Anger

Sometimes, people are not kind or fair. Anger is a healthy human feeling-response to such injustice. When someone treats us or others unfairly, we notice that we are strongly displeased. That displeasure is what is meant by anger. It can be expressed in violent or nonviolent ways. When we turn our anger into violence or revenge, it becomes abuse. When we express our anger in a mature way, we control our temper to avoid causing more harm. We do not fly off the handle; we calmly look at what's happening and then express our anger as a feeling-communication not as a threat of violence.

The process for releasing our anger in a mature and respectful way is very simple: we declare it aloud and directly. We do so as a communication of a feeling not as a tactic to intimidate the person who offended us. Likewise, we do not seek revenge, cherish rancor, show ill will, or engage in blaming the other. In psychological health and spiritual maturity, we are sharing a feeling not punishing the one who has triggered us.

— 𝒾𝓁𝑒 —

My tongue will tell the anger of my heart,
Or else my heart, concealing it, will break. (*The Taming of the Shrew*, Act IV, Scene 3)

I have to express my anger; otherwise, I will be brokenhearted.

Be advised, heat not a furnace for your foe so hot, that it do singe yourself. (*Henry VIII*, Act I, Scene 1)

Make sure your rage is not so strong that you burn yourself.

How angrily I taught my brow to frown,
When inward joy enforced my heart to smile! (*Two Gentlemen of Verona*, Act I, Scene 2)

I tried to fend off the one I wanted by pretending to be angry, when inside me I was really attracted to him or her. I pushed away what most I wanted.

O gentle son,
Upon the heat and flame of thy distemper
Sprinkle cool patience. (*Hamlet*, Act III, Scene 4)

Let go of some of your anger by being more patient.

If the balance of our lives had not one
scale of reason to poise another of sensuality, the
blood and baseness of our natures would conduct us

to most preposterous conclusions: but we have
reason to cool our raging motions. (*Othello*, Act I, Scene 3)

We have a prefrontal cortex to call upon when our amygdala is trying to stage a coup! In other words, our rational mind can still intervene when our impulses are aroused.

Who can be wise, amazed, temperate and furious,
Loyal and neutral, in a moment? (*Macbeth*, Act II, Scene 3)

This passage shows us the reverse side of the above quotation from Othello. Fury can cancel access to reason.

— ﻌﻠ —

When we hold anger in, it can become smoldering resentment. Then we are choosing the path of alienation from the other and of ongoing stress to ourselves. In other words, anger can't be held in if we want to maintain our relationships and be healthy ourselves; no feeling can. Repression is a cause of suffering.

At the same time, we are not carried off by the emotion of anger, but only express it so that it appropriately matches the injustice that has happened. In spiritual consciousness, we maintain a sense of compassion for ourselves and for the person who has acted in a way that upset the balance between us. The social contract that healthy humans are committed to includes acting fairly. When this does not happen, our spiritual commitment is to respond in ways that are not abusive.

Our feeling is our own responsibility. What others do is a catalyst not a cause of our feeling. People can trigger us, but they can't make us react in any specific way; the way we react is our choice. Since most of us react in primitive ways, we need a spiritual practice to keep us on track. That "track" is to be assertive rather than adopting either the passivity of a victim or the aggression of an enemy.

In the quotation above from *Two Gentlemen of Verona*, we see an option we might not guess could happen: we sometimes feel drawn to someone erotically but don't want to admit it. We act aggressively toward that person to keep him or her at arm's length, when all the while we want connection. We are using a frown to hide a smile we dare not display. What complex and contrary beings we are!

5

Confronting Our Fears

The feeling of fear is our body's way of warning us about a danger or threat. At the same time, we take on unsubstantiated fears. For instance, we may fear closeness in a relationship when such a threat is not reality-based.

Many of our fears, real or imagined, are inherited from childhood and stored in every cell of our bodies. Likewise, we may have experienced traumas, harmful invasions of our boundaries, physical or emotional abuses, woundings at many levels of our emotional being and physical body. We may carry these fears and traumas, often unnamed, into our adulthood. We may be holding anxieties that plague and rob us of serenity and reduce our self-esteem.

Fear sometimes becomes our go-to. Imagination can be the handmaid of neurotic fear. No matter what happens, we imagine the direst of consequences. We expect the worst. We bring fear into our experience of what is new or challenging. We might even fear losing what we love or what we cling to. In fact, we fear being unable to handle what may happen more than we fear what may happen.

Sometimes our fears are more than automatic reflexes. They might be examples of post-traumatic stress. We are associating events in the present with abuses from the past. Fear is an expert at disguises. Our amygdala, a primitive part of our emotional brain that stores fears and memories, does not distinguish past from present, so the danger from long ago presents itself as real now.

— ﺓ —

Be not afear'd; the isle is full of noises,
Sounds and sweet airs, that give delight and hurt not. (*The Tempest*, Act III, Scene 2)

Never fear natural sounds in nature; they are really songs that can bring us joy.

In time we hate that which we often fear. (*Antony and Cleopatra*, Act I, Scene 3)

Eventually, we will hate those things and people we fear.

Swift, swift, you dragons of the night, that dawning
May bare the raven's eye! I lodge in fear;
Though this a heavenly angel, hell is here. (*Cymbeline*, Act II, Scene 2)

As long as I am afraid, I am in hell no matter what the surrounding reality.

Such tricks hath strong imagination
That if it would but apprehend some joy,
It comprehends some bringer of that joy,
Or, in the night, imagining some fear,
How easy is a bush supposed a bear! (*A Midsummer's Night Dream*, Act V, Scene 1)

WHO ARE WE?

Our wishful thinking makes us believe that, if we can think of happiness, there must be some provider of it. At other times, our fear-based imagination can make us afraid of something that is harmless.

Present fears
Are less than horrible imaginings. (*Macbeth*, Act I, Scene 2)

Our reality-based fears are less threatening than our imaginary fears. The mind is more a source of stress than reality is.

Be not afraid of shadows. (*Richard III*, Act V, Scene 3)

Don't be scared by your own fantasies of what may seem dangerous.

Alas, it is the baseness of thy fear
That makes thee strangle thy propriety [deny your identity].
    (*Twelfth Night*, Act V, Scene 1)

Overpowering fear deceives us into believing we are less powerful than we are.

Our doubts are traitors
And make us lose the good we oft might win
By fearing to attempt. (*Measure for Measure*, Act I, Scene 4)

Our self-doubts or mistrust make us lose heart and prevent us from achieving what we want because we are afraid to try.

We hear this fearful tempest sing,
Yet see no shelter to avoid the storm;
We see the wind sit sore upon our sails,
And yet we strike not, but securely perish. (*Richard II*, Act II,
    Scene 10)

At times, we may be aware of a threat but find no refuge from it or not when action is needed.

— ❧ —

Fear is a bully that can make us doubt our own inner strength. We lose our self-confidence when we are in the grip of fear. When we are faced with a crisis, fear stymies and shackles us. We lose faith in our own powers. Then events may overwhelm us. Our vulnerability to self-doubt is a touching fact about us. When we look deeply into what is going on within us, we may realize that we actually fear our own power. We keep a diminished portrait of ourselves in the locket that hangs around our neck like a chain. In fact, we have capacities to handle what happens. If we can't believe that, then we can at least *act as if* we "had power all along" as Glinda said to Dorothy in *The Wizard of Oz*.

When we equate the unknown, the untried, and the unfamiliar with fear, it becomes a tyrant ruling our life and decisions. We have become victims of our fears. Likewise, we may destabilize when things fall apart or when a traumatic event occurs. We feel lost, ungrounded, and without any reliable inner resources. Then we may become paranoid—our body on red alert and our mind creating fictions. The fears that then rush in are not real; they are the results of the destabilization. We are looking into our fears and believing they are accurately depicting reality. Indeed, unsubstantiated neurotic fear is always the exact opposite of fidelity to reality. Such fears show us what we falsely imagine and not what is real.

We may believe that, if we stay in control, we will stave off fear. Paradoxically, as we let go of control in favor of a yes to what it is, we are letting go of fear too. Saying yes is surrendering to reality without resistance or reservation. It is then that I bow to what is, just this, just now. This is what true fidelity to reality is—a fast track to freedom from the grip of fear. We will fear all

35

our lives so there is no freedom from fear, but there is a chance to release ourselves from its deadly clench.

Ways to Handle Fear

Things done well,
And with a care, exempt themselves from fear. (*Henry VIII*, Act
   II, Scene 2)

When we feel contented that we have done something well, we automatically notice we have nothing left to fear.

'Tis much he dares,
And to that dauntless temper of his mind
He hath a wisdom that doth guide his valor
To act in safety. (*Macbeth*, Act III, Scene 1)

Here, Macbeth is saying of Banquo: He is courageous enough to take risks and has the kind of wisdom that keeps him safe as he does so.

Be that thou know'st thou art and then thou art as great as that
   thou fear'st. (*Twelfth Night*, Act V, Scene 1)

Be yourself and you become equal to your fear and thus overcome it.

Fear no more the frown of the great,
Thou art past the tyrant's stroke. (*Cymbeline*, Act III, Scene 7)

Don't fear the mighty; you are an adult now and past their power to harm you.

There is no terror, Cassius, in your threats,
For I am armed so strong in honesty

Confronting Our Fears

That they pass by me as the idle wind,
Which I respect not. (*Julius Caesar*, Act IV, Scene 3)

Your threats are powerless over me because my own integrity makes them fall flat.

That life is better life, past fearing death,
Than that which lives to fear. (*Measure for Measure*, Act V,
    Scene 1)

Our life is a lot better without fear especially when we are no longer afraid of death.

It is more worthy to leap in ourselves,
Than tarry till they push us. (*Julius Caesar*, Act V, Scene 5)

It is more laudable to take a big leap of our own volition than to be pushed into it by others.

Though the seas threaten, they are merciful. (*The Tempest*, Act
    V, Scene 1)

No matter how menacing something is, there is always an opportunity for grace and release will be a chance for release.

Stand, stand! We have the advantage of the ground;
The lane is guarded: nothing routs us but
The villainy of our fears. (*Cymbeline*, Act V, Scene 2)

Nothing can defeat us except the pernicious bully of fear.

The good I stand on is my truth and honesty:
If they shall fail, I, with mine enemies,
Will triumph o'er my person; which I weigh not,
Being of those virtues vacant. I fear nothing
What can be said against me. (*Henry VIII*, Act V, Scene 1)

WHO ARE WE?

I hold onto my virtues, and therefore, do not fear rumors about or judgments of me.

— ﷴ —

We may never be free of unreal fears, but we can be free of the obligation or compulsion to act on them. We can choose not to let fears stop us from doing what we need to do or push us to do what we don't want to do—or want to become.

Life is most fulfilling when we challenge the power that fear insists it has over us. We then can stand up to fear. We can do this in many ways. For instance, we can act with integrity and loving-kindness, builders of self-esteem, in all our dealings. We soon notice that conscience conquers self-deception; we see— and love—ourselves as we are. This is a pathway to freedom from fear.

On that path, we might notice a wonderful grace opening within us: we are no longer under the spell of fear. This includes the sense of satisfaction and self-appreciation that goes with doing something well. As we act efficaciously and fulfill our life goals— other building blocks of self-esteem—we become less anxious. We have found fearlessness in ourselves just as we are.

Fear leads us ordinarily to fight or flee, sometimes to freeze. A healing alternative is to relate to our fear. We do this when we follow this three-step practice. First, we admit to ourselves and someone we trust that we are afraid. Second, we let ourselves feel our fear fully, rather than hiding from it with distractions such as substances, self-deception, wishful thinking. These two steps lead us to step three: to act as if fear could not stop us from doing what we need to do nor drive us to do what we don't really want to do.*

---

* This topic is developed further in my book *When Love Meets Fear: Becoming Defenseless and Resource-full*, rev. ed. (Mahwah, NJ: Paulist Press, 2022).

6

Our Shadow Side

Carl Jung spoke of an unconscious "shadow side" in each of us containing the opposite attitudes and behaviors of the persona we show to the world. The "negative shadow" refers to our capacity to act in self-centered, harming, or even malicious ways. We also have a capacity to act in gifted and benevolent ways— what Jung called our "positive shadow side." Both capacities are hidden in our unconscious. We may not believe we really can be as bad as the worst we have seen in others or as good as the best we have seen in others. But we each have both capacities.

In childhood, we may have been taught that it is dangerous to act in certain ways that society or our family would regard as anti-social. We may then have denied and disavowed these tendencies rather than humbly acknowledge them and choose not to act on them.

However, we may have been belittled into the false belief that we possessed no value, virtue, or talent and taught that we were useless to ourselves and others. We may have been told that we would never amount to anything, causing us to doubt or deny our talents and gifts, for fear of opening our own original blessings, of releasing—or even knowing—the full spectrum of our human powers. The challenge is to accept ourselves fully—from the positive top and to the negative bottom.

Plays more often focus on dark deeds so, in the quotations below, there will be more emphasis placed on the negative shadow than on the positive shadow.

— 𝔢 —

Affairs, that walk,
As they say spirits do, at midnight, have
In them a wilder nature than the business
That seeks dispatch by day. (*Henry VIII*, Act V, Scene 1)

The dark side has creative powers that we abjure in the daylight of consciousness.

Where's that palace whereinto foul things
Sometimes intrude not? (*Othello*, Act III, Scene 3)

Every institution—or person—has a dark side no matter how good the person or thing appears to be.

Oh, that deceit should steal such gentle shapes,
And with a virtuous visage hide foul guile! (*Richard III*, Act II, Scene 2)

We are deceived sometimes by what looks good externally and we fail to see the hidden shadow side.

Was ever book containing such vile matter
So fairly bound? O that deceit should dwell
In such a gorgeous palace! (*Romeo and Juliet*, Act III, Scene 2)

What looks really good can be concealing what is not so good.

Our Shadow Side

O, that estates, degrees, and offices
Were not derived corruptly, and that clear honor
Were purchased by the merit of the wearer! (*Merchant of Venice*,
     Act II, Scene 9)

*It is unfortunate that ranks can be gained in corrupt ways. Would
that honors were based only on merit!*

…oftentimes, to win us to our harm,
The instruments of darkness tell us truths,
Win us with honest trifles, to betray us
In deepest consequence. (*Macbeth*, Act I, Scene 3)

*Sometimes, the forces of evil fool us with what seems to be a truth so
we end up doing darker deeds.*

Men's natures wrangle with inferior things,
Though great ones are their object. (*Othello*, Act III, Scene 4)

*We get caught up in minutiae when our real destiny is to accomplish
greater things.*

It is a heretic that makes the fire,
Not she which burns in it. (*The Winter's Tale*, Act I, Scene 3)

*The real sinner, the one who doesn't believe in divine love, is the
person who judges and punishes those who are different.*

The web of our life is of a mingled yarn, good and ill together:
     our virtues would be proud if our faults whipped them not;
     and our crimes would despair, if they were not cherished by
     our virtues. (*All's Well that Ends Well*, Act IV, Scene 3)

It is a given that we will meet with both good and ill in and outside ourselves. If we were always virtuous, we might become conceited; if we were always immoral, we might despair.

I say, there is no darkness but ignorance… (*Twelfth Night*, Act IV, Scene2)

It is our willful ignorance that keeps us from the light of truth. (This quotation is inscribed on the statue of Shakespeare in Leicester Square, Central London.)

— ⚓ —

We are not fooled by the externals of people or institutions. We know that all people, including us, have a negative shadow side. Sometimes, the dark forces can hoodwink us because they appear in the guise of what seems appropriate or valuable, but in fact, they are dangerous. We might even be cajoled into doing what is wrong by the trickster-shadow energy that makes wrong look right.

The challenge is to see and accept the given of life that all people present a persona, what they want us to believe about them. This persona may be strongly appealing. Yet, it is also a given of life that we all have a face behind our persona that does not match the sterling qualities we see. Emily Dickinson describes this twofold identity in the fourth stanza of her poem "One need not be a chamber to be haunted":

Ourself, behind ourself concealed,
Should startle most;
Assassin, hid in our apartment,
Be horror's least.*

Finally, Shakespeare reminds us of a spiritual teaching. When

_____

* Emily Dickinson, https://www.public-domain-poetry.com.

we punish others for their actions, we are breaking human connection. We are not loving our fellow humans to our full spiritual capacity, that is, unconditionally. We are giving up on them, when the holy Spirit of love never does.

Befriending Our Shadow Side

It is very much lamented, Brutus,
That you have no such mirrors as will turn
Your hidden worthiness into your eye,
That you might see your shadow. (*Julius Caesar*, Act I, Scene 2)

It is a shame that you don't fully acknowledge your own self.

Happy are they who hear their distractions and can put them to
     mending. (*Much Ado About Nothing*, Act II, Scene 3)

*It is a wonderful quality to be open to feedback about our faults and
then to mend them.*

For naught so vile that on the earth doth live
But to the earth some special good doth give,
Nor aught so good but strain'd from that fair use
Revolts from true birth, stumbling on abuse:
Virtue itself turns vice, being misapplied;
And vice sometimes by action dignified. (*Romeo and Juliet*, Act
     II, Scene 3)

*There is nothing on earth that is so evil that it does not provide the
earth with some special quality. And there is nothing that does not turn
bad if it is put to the wrong use. Virtue turns to vice if it's misused, and
vice sometimes becomes virtue through right behavior.*

WHO ARE WE?

This thing of darkness I acknowledge mine. (*The Tempest*, Act V, Scene 1)

I acknowledge my own shadow side when I see it in someone else.

There is some soul of goodness in things evil
When men observingly distill it out. (*Henry V*, Act IV, Scene 1)

We can always find good in evil if we look closely enough.

— ॐ —

We can integrate our shadow side by being self-compassionate and befriending it. We can understand that having a dark side does not render us helpless nor is it a sign that we are bad people. We all have the capacity for wrongdoing. We can acknowledge that and choose to act in ways that move us toward goodness. Thereby we are adapting our inner capacities to our life purpose, to co-create a world in which love is more our style of behaving and being.

As we noted above, the dark side has creative energies trapped in it. As we acknowledge our own shadow side rather than project it onto others, we find creative ore in its grim caves. For instance, we may not see that we are controlling and even strongly react to controlling behavior in others. We dislike and condemn them for it. Yet, if we admit that we can also be controlling and manipulative, we might locate wonderful powers in those behaviors: the ability to get things done, good follow-through, and leadership. These are creative energies implicit in the controlling behavior. They are trapped while they are projected onto others and not acknowledged in ourselves, for instance, by admitting our own controlling behavior. As we have noted, any negative trait hides a valuable kernel within it. We are more likely to show our golden self when we acknowledge our leaden ego.

Likewise, and more positively, when we idealize and overly admire others, we can come to see that we too must have similar gifts. Unconsciously, we are projecting our own positive capacities onto others. Our work is to trust that their gifts are also in us and then to cultivate them. We befriend ourselves when we find in ourselves what we so admire in others. In *The Spectrum of Consciousness*, Ken Wilbur wrote, "We build pedestals out of our own untapped potential." In other words, we honor the capacities in others that are hidden in ourselves. This also applies to our veneration of saints. When we look fervently at a picture of St. Francis, we are gazing into a mirror of our own disavowed saintliness.

In both the negative and positive dimensions of our humanness, we see that, in accepting ourselves fully—light and shadow—we amplify our opportunity to act creatively.

7

The Gift of Joy

The Merriam-Webster dictionary defines *joy* as "the emotion evoked by well-being, success, good fortune, or by the prospect of having what one desires." Joy is not a feeling we can muster on our own. It is an automatic result of a positive experience.

Joy in the Christian tradition is a grace from the Holy Spirit, the divine source of love, wisdom, courage, and joy. This view goes beyond the dictionary definition: Spiritual joy is our secure sense of God within and around us. Joy comes as a gift that also fills us with the optimism that good will ultimately triumph over evil in the world. In this sense, joy is our foundation of hope that there will be a positive outcome to human history. The mystic Juliana of Norwich must have felt this when she wrote, "All will be well."

In Shakespeare's *Henry VI, Part 2*, the king uses the expression: "the treasury of everlasting joy" (Act II, Scene 1). From a Jungian perspective, each of us has access to a vast collective human treasury of wisdom, healing, virtue, and enlightenment. In this context, our joy is based on that realization. Additionally, the joy of all humans, like the grief of all humans, is experienced both individually and collectively. When we mourn, we are one with mourners the world over. When we are happy, we join in the happiness of all humanity, past and present. Thus, joy is bigger than any of us and shows the bigness in all of us.

Finally, joy is more than pleasure. The two differ even physically. Pleasure is aroused by dopamine, the hormone of reward; joy is activated by oxytocin, the hormone of warmth and comfort. Dopamine gives us immediate satisfaction. Oxytocin gives us a sense of security based on a caring connection, the very definition of love. This is how joy is and creates a oneness between us and the human community, the very definition of the divine.

— ☙ —

And frame your mind to mirth and merriment,
Which bars a thousand harms and lengthens life. (*The Taming of the Shrew*, Act I, Scene 2)

A joyful mood builds our immune system and makes for a long life.

Where joy most revels, grief doth most lament;
Grief joys, joy grieves, on slender accident. (*Hamlet*, Act III, Scene 2)

Sadness can turn into joy, and vice-versa, with even the slightest twist of fate.

With mirth and laughter let old wrinkles come. (*The Merchant of Venice*, Act I, Scene 1)

It is not a problem for me if laughing causes wrinkles.

Silence is the perfectest herald of joy: I were but little happy,
if I could say how much. (*Much Ado about Nothing*, Act II, Scene 1)

WHO ARE WE?

In the fullness of joy, we are rendered speechless. If I were only partially happy, I could express it in words.

Sir, I am a true laborer: I earn that I eat, get
that I wear, owe no man hate, envy no man's
happiness, glad of other men's good, content with my
harm, and the greatest of my pride is to see my ewes
graze and my lambs suck. (*As You Like It*, Act III, Scene 2)

I am a simple workman. I earn my food and clothing; I don't hate anyone; I don't envy anyone's happiness; I am happy about others' good fortune; I accept my own misfortune; and my greatest sense of pride comes from seeing my ewes grazing and my lambs feeding.

Although assailed with fortune fierce and keen,
Virtue preserved from fell destruction's blast,
Led on by heaven, and crowned with joy at last…. (*Pericles*, Act
    V, Scene 3)

Despite harsh misfortune, we maintained our virtue, led by divine guidance, and are rejoicing at last.

Well, I will forget the condition of my estate, rejoice in yours.
    (*As You Like It*, Act I, Scene 2)

I rejoice in your good fortune even when I am sad about my predicament.

Ah, Juliet, if the measure of thy joy
Be heaped like mine and that thy skill be more
To blazon it, then sweeten with thy breath
This neighbor air, and let rich music's tongue
Unfold the imagined happiness that both
Receive in either by this dear encounter. (*Romeo and Juliet*, Act
    II, Scene 6)

The Gift of Joy

Juliet, if you are as delighted as I am about our love, declare with art of your speech the happiness that we will enjoy from one another.

With all my heart; and much it joys me too,
To see you are become so penitent. (*Richard III*, Act I, Scene 2)

I am content to see you take responsibility for your actions and show contrition for wrongs.

Then is there mirth in heaven,
When earthly things made even
Atone together. (*As You Like It*, Act V, Scene 4)

God is happy when things come into balance and people connect. The word "atone" is used to convey the meaning of "at one" not make amends.

— ☾ —

Here are five major features of joy:

- Joy contributes to our health and well-being. It also feels like a protection from harm since it builds our inner resources and defenses. Shakespeare's words "frame our mind" are the same as our modern realization that "we can create new neural pathways in our brain." This happens when we find a jubilant dimension in our circumstances and choices.
- The most enduring joy comes from the acceptance of life as it is—showing love and not hate, being content with our simplest daily work and activities. Personal adversities cannot shake that kind of joy.
- Our happiness in a relationship is based on our mutual love that we show unconditionally. In fact, unconditional love is a cause and sustainer of lasting joy.

- When others offend us, we are happy to see their contrition and penitence. Shakespeare states this idea clearly in *The Tempest*: "They being penitent, / The sole drift of my purpose doth extend / Not a frown further" (*The Tempest*, Act V, Scene 1). Likewise, and by grace, to forgive those who trespass against us is a path to a divine gladness indeed.

- We can experience what the mystics call "quiet joy." We do not have to be boisterous or even verbal about our feeling of delight. Silence deepens us so that we see into the meaning of our own reality. Joy, too, can partake of this contemplative silence. Such joy comes to us in a moment, and yet we intuit that it was always in us. Pierre Teilhard de Chardin expresses a similar idea: "A glorious unsuspected feeling of joy invaded my soul."*

---

* Pierre Teilhard de Chardin, *Writings in Time of War* (London: Collins, 1968).

8

Knowing and Showing
Our True Self

In coming to know our true self, we recognize that we have a unique inborn psychological makeup. We also see that some of our traits, like our physical DNA, are inherited from family members. Additionally, our true self includes the treasury of wisdom and archetypal energies that we have inherited from the human collective, our ancient unknown ancestry.

We find our true self when we look at who we were from the beginning of our lives before we became obedient to the plans that others had for us. The false self is the persona that we learned early on was the only safe one to show to the world around us. For instance, we might be highly introverted but our enmeshing family with all its dramas demanded that we act in extraverted ways. Later, we may keep acting that way, believing that it is the only way to get people to like us. Someday, hopefully, we come to appreciate and accept ourselves as the introverts we are, and we design our life accordingly. Do we truly reflect our deepest needs, values, and wishes in our daily life or what others want us to be? Freedom to be ourselves entails an expression of our true self revealed without reserve—at least to those we trust.

Most of us have forgotten the look of our true face. We thereby fail to believe we have the powers that come with it. Perhaps these two words from *Measure for Measure* describe our predicament best: "unknown sovereignty" (Act V, Scene 1). Our journey is to rediscover the treasure of our sovereignty.

— ﻉﻟ —

My thoughts are whirled like a potter's wheel; I know not where
    I am, nor what I do. (*Henry VI, Part One*, Act I, Scene 5)

I am so confused that I don't know where I am or what my true choice is.

Go to your bosom;
Knock there, and ask your heart what it doth know…. (*Measure for Measure*, Act II, Scene 2)

Look into your heart for wisdom especially about who you are.

What my tongue dares not, that my heart shall say. (*Richard II*, Act V, Scene 5)

I may be afraid to speak up, but my heart is telling me the truth without hesitation or fear.

It may be so; but yet my inward soul
Persuades me it is otherwise. (*Richard II*, Act II, Scene 2)

Sometimes our intuition gives us an accurate report on reality no matter what we may see or hear.

Knowing and Showing Our True Self

There's no art
To find the mind's construction in the face. (*Macbeth*, Act I,
    Scene 4)

There is no way to know a person just from his face. In other words,
"we can't judge a book by its cover."

You have but mistook me all this while. (*Richard II*, Act III,
    Scene 2)

You have failed to see my true self all this time.

Presume not that I am the thing I was.... (*Henry IV*, *Part Two*,
    Act V, Scene 5)

I am not now who I once was.

Yet...
My perfect soul
Shall manifest me rightly. (*Othello*, Act I, Scene 2)

I trust a soul quality that will portray to the world what I truly am.

Now I will unmask. (*Measure for Measure*, Act V, Scene 1)

I will now show myself just as I am.

I have unclasped
To thee the book even of my secret soul. (*Twelfth Night*, Act I
    Scene 4)

I have shared the deepest part of me with you.

This above all: to thine own self be true,
And it must follow, as the night the day,
Thou canst not then be false to any man. (*Hamlet*, Act I, Scene 3)

WHO ARE WE?

Be true to who you really are, and you will thereby be true to and respectful of who others are.

...daffodils,
That come before the swallow dares... (*The Winter's Tale*, Act IV, Scene 3)

I admire the daffodils, which take a chance and show themselves at winter before the swallow dares make an appearance.

— ॐ —

Some people know us; some don't get us at all. We sometimes know ourselves and at other times can't understand ourselves, our attitudes, or our behavior. No matter what, we can affirm that we will be candid about ourselves, our needs, and our longings. We will then want all that we do and say to portray our authentic self. We will be glad when people catch us in the act of being who we really are. We will not be keeping up appearances. We will want to be seen just as we are.

Knowing and showing our true self focuses us more on what really matters spiritually: how who we are can benefit all beings. People around us, even our near and dear, may not really know us. They may mistake our intentions and motivations. They may not believe we have changed when we have. We can willingly accept this as one of life's givens. Such acceptance leads us to a simple practice: explain ourselves and, at the same time, let go of having to be fully understood.

In any case, it is scary for many of us to show others our deepest needs, values, and wishes. We may feel vulnerable knowing that others might shame us for who we are; they might take advantage of our honesty and use it against us. Ultimately, we can only self-disclose when we have the courage to handle the reactions of others. Only then is our showing the world who we are and what we want more valuable than how others react to us. We are glad that we have become who we are and that we are letting others know us that way. That healthy pride sustains us with the serenity to accept that some people will love us for who we are and that others will not. Our courage has made it easy to say yes to either response with an amused shrug or a humble bow.

Part Two

What
Happens
to Us

9

When Things Change

In *The Western Canon: The Books and School of the Ages*, Harold Bloom writes, "Shakespeare surpasses all others in evidencing a psychology of mutability." Change is one given of human existence that no one can doubt. Most of us want everything good to remain so. Yet, we have no control over how things change. It is optimistic—and useful—to view change as evolutionary. We then appreciate phases of life and relationship as having a positive developmental arc. We trust change as a challenge to grow and expand our horizons as well as our inner resources. When we see the given of change as an opportunity for personal evolution, we no longer fear it. We welcome change as a given of life and trust ourselves to its challenges.

A central teaching in Buddhism is impermanence. Since all is transitory, our wisest attitude is acceptance of, rather than clinging to, what is passing. In ancient Rome, triumphant generals returning to the city were shown a flash of fire with an utterance of the words "*Sic transit gloria mundi*" (This is how fast worldly glory passes). In the traditional coronation of popes, a flare was lit while those same words were spoken to the pope elect. We don't have to lose hope when we experience transitoriness. We reply,

WHAT HAPPENS TO US

"Yes, now what?" This practice combines radical acceptance and a moving on to what awaits us in the new landscape we behold. Mary, queen of Scots, in her last words, said it well: "In my end is my beginning."

— ه —

Men shut their doors against a setting sun. (*Timon of Athens*, Act I, Scene 2)

We fight the fact of impermanence trying so hard to deny it when it is happening right here in front of us.

To-morrow, and to-morrow, and to-morrow,
Creeps in this petty pace from day to day,
To the last syllable of recorded time;
And all our yesterdays have lighted fools
The way to dusty death. Out, out, brief candle!
Life's but a walking shadow, a poor player
That struts and frets his hour upon the stage
And then is heard no more. It is a tale
Told by an idiot, full of sound and fury
Signifying nothing. (*Macbeth*, Act 5, Scene 5)

Everything is transitory. Our life is full of worries that end—as do we. There is much hoopla but no ultimate meaning.

Injurious time now with a robber's haste
Crams his rich thievery up, he knows not how:
As many farewells as be stars in heaven,
With distinct breath and consign'd kisses to them,
He fumbles up into a lose adieu,
And scants us with a single famish'd kiss,
Distasted with the salt of broken tears. (*Troilus and Cressida*, Act IV, Scene 4)

When Things Change

Time runs away quickly with our lives like a thief who steals something but without knowing its full value. What is truly precious he leaves behind. All we get is a brief kiss and even that is ruined by the salt in our tears.

For time is like a fashionable host
That slightly shakes his parting guest by the hand,
And with his arms outstretched, as he would fly,
Grasps in the comer: welcome ever smiles,
And farewell goes out sighing. (*Troilus and Cressida*, Act III,
    Scene 3)

Time is fickle, welcoming in as he ushers out.

All the world's a stage,
And all the men and women merely players,
They have their exits and entrances,
And one man in his time plays many parts,
His acts being seven ages. At first the infant,
Mewling and puking in the nurse's arms.
Then, the whining schoolboy with his satchel
And shining morning face, creeping like snail
Unwillingly to school. And then the lover,
Sighing like furnace, with a woeful ballad
Made to his mistress' eyebrow. Then a soldier,
Full of strange oaths, and bearded like the pard,
Jealous in honor, sudden, and quick in quarrel,
Seeking the bubble reputation
Even in the cannon's mouth. And then the justice
In fair round belly, with good capon lin'd,
With eyes severe, and beard of formal cut,
Full of wise saws, and modern instances,
And so he plays his part. The sixth age shifts
Into the lean and slippered pantaloon,

WHAT HAPPENS TO US

With spectacles on nose, and pouch on side,
His youthful hose well saved, a world too wide,
For his shrunk shank, and his big manly voice,
Turning again towards childish treble, pipes
And whistles in his sound. Last scene of all,
That ends this strange eventful history,
Is second childishness and mere oblivion,
Sans teeth, sans eyes, sans taste, sans everything. (*As You Like It*,
   Act II, Scene 7)

*Actors play many parts, and so do we. The roles reflect the phases
of our aging from birth to death. None of them last; each one yields to
the next in an ineluctable, inescapable sequence and we are left with
nothing.*

The wheel is come full circle: I am here. (*King Lear*, Act V,
   Scene 3)

I have gone through seasons of change, and I am back where I began.

O momentary grace of mortal men,
Which we more hunt for than the grace of God! (*Richard III*,
   Act III, Scene 4)

*We seek gifts from others that are fleeting more than divine graces
that are enduring.*

Oh! You gods, why do you make us love your goodly gifts, and
   snatch them straight away? (*Pericles*, Act III, Scene 1)

*We shake our fist at heaven that good things granted us are so quickly
snatched away.*

When Things Change

We can go through phases of life as nature passes gracefully through seasons. Each season has a purpose and a connection to the others. Likewise, our psychological and spiritual seasons have a way of upgrading our connections with the world and with others. As children, we trust others unconditionally; as adults, we trust those who prove themselves trustworthy and become trustworthy toward others as part of our spiritual practice.

We also can't help but notice that our wonderful gifts and talents go through phases. We excelled at sports in our younger days, for instance, but now our bodies don't permit us to play as energetically or for as long as we did before. We can't blame God or nature for this; our bodies are going through phases of aging. We are being readied for a more serene style in the world, for quieter arts. We get the message from our body and move in new ways.

Each of us lives in the center of a square room with a picture window on each wall. The east window faces the rising sun and shows us what is coming up for us. The west window faces the setting sun and shows us what we need to let go of. The window of southern exposure, full of warmth and light, evokes serenity as well as creativity and spontaneity. The north window faces the north star and shows us what to rely on, our spiritual go-to, and what grounds and guides us. Thinking of our life as one long day, our practice is to turn and face each window with a yes. We are the sunflower gladly turning with earth and sun. Beginnings, endings, comforts, guideposts—all four are welcome. When we live in this roomy and acceptant way, our fear of change turns into excitement about change—the true destination of all our fears.

10

The Mystery of Time

Time is the word we find most frequently in Shakespeare's writings. He keeps coming back to the contemplation of time without ever coming up with a conclusion. Yet, he seems to bow often to its inherent mystery.

We can understand why time might have primacy in the human imagination. It is mysterious in how it passes, in what it can bring and take away, and in how it changes us and everything. Time is also relative and, therefore, feels unreliable. Sometimes, it seems to move too slowly; sometimes, it seems to fly by. But the deepest mystery of time is how it gives and takes all at once. On the day of our birth, we are given a lifetime; and on the day our death, our time here comes to an end. It is an advanced spiritual practice to honor this mystery, embracing both ends of the spectrum of life and everything in between with equal acceptance.

What does acceptance really require of us? We cultivate an attitude of hospitality to what time presents to us. We gently grant a hospice to what time takes from us.

We trust that time has a healing quality, and we feel gratitude for that. We notice that some traumas do not yield to time, and we honor that predicament. We notice that the passing of time helps us to see more clearly and deeply. For this too we are thankful. We notice that sometimes time obfuscates and muddles our sense of what is real. We accept this as a given of life while at the same time doing all we can to find a clear path to our own truth.

Now, time may have affected our memory, and we resign ourselves to the loss while not giving up on ourselves. When we befriend the vicissitudes of time they turn into *seasons*. We now feel the joy of experiencing time as Mother Nature does—as the adventure of evolving.

— ꙰ —

What else may hap, to time I will commit. (*Twelfth Night*, Act I
    Scene 2)

What else may happen next, I leave to time.

…what needful else
That calls upon us, by the grace of Grace,
We will perform in measure, time and place…. (*Macbeth*, Act V,
    Scene 8)

We intend to do all we need to do at the right time and the right place.

…we intended
To keep in darkness what occasion now
Reveals before 'tis ripe. (*Twelfth Night*, Act V Scene 1)

We intended to keep secret until the right moment what has suddenly been discovered before we wanted it to be revealed.

How poor are they that have not patience!
What wound did ever heal but by degrees? (*Othello*, Act II,
    Scene 3)

65

WHAT HAPPENS TO US

We lose so much when we are not patient. It takes time for our wounds to heal. Patience is a catalyst to accessing our healing powers.

True hope is swift, and flies with swallow's wings. (*Richard III,*
    Act III, Scene 5)

We can trust that hope will sweep in quickly.

Put not yourself into amazement how these
things should be: all difficulties are but easy
when they are known. (*Measure for Measure*, Act IV, Scene 2)

Don't be puzzled by what is happening. All complications become clear when we see what caused them.

I see that Time's the king of men.
He's both their parent, and he is their grave,
And gives them what he will, not what they crave. (*Pericles,*
    Act II, Scene 3)

Time passes and gives or takes not based on what we will or want but on his whim.

There's some ill planet reigns:
I must be patient till the heavens look
With an aspect more favorable. (*The Winter's Tale*, Act II,
    Scene 1)

I can feel that the time is not right for this venture. I must wait till the stars align to favor what I want to have happen.

The time is out of joint—O cursed spite
That ever I was born to set it right. (*Hamlet*, Act I, Scene 5)

The Mystery of Time

This is not the time for things to work out and what a terrible burden that I am the one who must get it all on track.

O time thou must untangle this, not I.
It is too hard a knot for me to untie. (*Twelfth Night*, Act II,
    Scene 2)

This problem will take its own time to be resolved. It will not respond to my skills or wishes.

Scan this thing no further; leave it to time. (*Othello*, Act III,
    Scene 3)

Don't keep trying to figure this out. Time will tell.

— ॐ —

To trust the power of time is to honor the process of gestation, the time required for a birth to happen. This takes more than patience. It takes trust in what occurs in the world around us: We will have to trust what is unfolding when we are not in on its design. We will have to let the chips fall where they may, when we want them to fall always in a way that makes us win. We will have to trust bedrock reality, which does not always arrange itself in accord with our wishes. The human reply to time can only be yes.

Let's use an analogy. We can make dough at any time. We can knead the dough for as long as we want. In both these phases of making bread, we are in control. (Indeed, control is the opposite of having to await timing.) When the next phase begins—letting the bread rise—we are no longer in control. We do not even get to watch the rising happen. We cover the bowl of dough with a cloth so the mystery can unfold as is required: in the dark. We allow the dough to rise in its own time and for as long as it takes. Then comes the final stage of the bread-making, the baking, and again, we are not in control of the timing. This four-part process is a metaphor. Half of our ventures must yield to the power of timing—a proportion that I have seen happen many times in my own life and in the lives of others. Our spiritual practice is to honor a timing not designed by us. This may mean having to feel that we are tied in a knot when we are trying to figure out what to do. It may mean waiting to find out whom to trust. We did just that when we were waiting to be born.

11

Meaningful Coincidence

Synchronicity is a term coined by Carl Jung. As we noted earlier, it refers to meaningful coincidence, the mysterious moment in which apparent opposites connect like notes in a chord, a resource matches a challenge, or two similar events happen at once. The time is then just right for us to know what is happening and to take the action needed to move forward on our unique journey. Synchronicity can't be planned; it simply happens. When synchronicity occurs, we are touched with a feeling, sometimes eerie, that there is a power around us that is helping things happen for us—a help that comes to us from a higher power than ego.

Meaningful coincidences and surprising connections occur often in our daily lives, yet we can fail to appreciate how they can guide, warn, and confirm us on our path. Synchronicity appears not only in our daily lives but also in our intimate relationships. We see, for instance, how synchronicity accounts for how we meet the people and partners who will turn out to be important in our lives. Our parents' first meeting was the greatest synchronicity of our own lives!

WHAT HAPPENS TO US

In our daily experience, sometimes what feel like fateful events keep happening. We can learn to recognize and work with meaningful coincidences, uncontrollable events, and uncanny happenstances, as invitations both to psychological and spiritual progress. In a way, everything that happens to us, every moment of every day, every social or intimate interaction is synchronicity, since there is nothing and not one moment that do not provide us with an opportunity for enlightenment.

O, 'tis an accident that heaven provides! (*Measure for Measure*, Act IV, Scene 3)

This was an unwelcome event but one that is for the best, thanks to powers beyond us.

When these prodigies
Do so conjointly meet, let not men say
"These are their reasons; they are natural";
For, I believe, they are portentous things
Unto the climate that they point upon. (*Julius Caesar*, Act I, Scene 3)

When natural disasters congregate, they do so with a greater intent than chance and point to a disaster headed in our direction.

I find my zenith doth depend upon
A most auspicious star, whose influence
If now I court not, but omit, my fortunes
Will ever after droop. (*The Tempest*, Act I, Scene 2)

My star-approved success is ready to happen and, if I don't act, I will lose my chance at a beneficial result.

Meaningful Coincidence

There is a tide in the affairs of men.
Which, taken at the flood, leads on to fortune;
Omitted, all the voyage of their life
Is bound in shallows and in miseries.
On such a full sea are we now afloat,
And we must take the current when it serves,
Or lose our ventures. (*Julius Caesar*, Act IV, Scene 2)

Now is the time for committed action. If I lose this chance, I miss the opportunity altogether.

...we defy augury: there's a special
providence in the fall of a sparrow. If it be now,
'tis not to come; if it be not to come, it will be
now; if it be not now, yet it will come: the
readiness is all: since no man has aught of what he
leaves, what is it to leave betimes [soon]? (*Hamlet*, Act V,
    Scene 2)

We can trust a power that comes to help us and a timing that works in our favor. At the same time, things happen beyond our control. All that matters is that we are ready.

Things growing are not ripe until their season
So I, being young, till now ripe not to reason;
And touching now the point of human skill,
Reason becomes the marshal to my will. (*A Midsummer's Night's
    Dream*, Act II, Scene 2)

I was too young to listen to reason; now I am of an age to be guided by it. A coincidence needs to happen between age and wise reasoning— and it does.

71

WHAT HAPPENS TO US

We can only make changes or experience transformation when we are ready. Some mysterious force beyond our cognitional powers lets us know exactly when the time is right for a particular move. We can set a goal and it will take time to achieve it. But if the time—right timing—has not kicked in, our efforts fall flat. This is all part of the mystery of time and its relation to timeliness, of which synchronicity is made. The light is only green when the time is right for it to be so. The light stays red when the time is not right, no matter how eager we are to make our move.

Synchronicity shows us that there is more to our psyche than is contained in our cranium. We realize that there is one coin of life—one side, the interior; the other, the exterior—but only one coin after all, no separation, no dualism. We find this one coin in ourselves and everywhere in three main ways:

- The first way is to respond in kind to the synchronicities that happen in our lives. For instance, a series of losses moves us to let go. A series of challenges moves us to take hold. We are now riding in the direction the horse is going.
- A second way is to find the oneness of ourselves and the world around us is to become witnesses of what happens. We do this when we move beyond what in Buddhism is called a cause of suffering: We no longer cling to what attracts us or reject what does not appeal to us. We simply notice all of it and get on with our lives.
- The third way is through deep meditation. We sit and breathe into a state of stillness and openness. When we do that—or rather, are that—the linear thinking centers of the brain go offline: "I am not solid now but fluid, so I flow with the universe in oneness." *Can I be silent long enough to tune in to divine silence?*

12

Fate and Chance

We are dragged along by fate to that inescapable goal we might have reached walking upright.

—Carl Jung, *Collected Works*, vol. 11

Fate usually refers to what is forced on us, while destiny is the fulfillment of our life journey, reachable by a combination of personal work and grace. We combine our own diligence with the gift dimension of the universe, grace, and thereby live out our calling. This provides us with a motivation for embarking on the daring expedition that is our life. The spiritual fulfillment of our human journey can be co-creating a world of justice, peace, and love.

We may believe that there is an inescapable fate that manipulates our life no matter what we do. We sense that what we think of as personal freedom is, in fact, severely limited by powers that pull the strings of the characters on; what Lear calls our "stage of fools" (*King Lear*, Act IV, Scene 6). Indeed, our ego fools itself with grandiose surveys of its liberty. Yet, we can't deny that certain events happen that could not be otherwise, no matter what we might have done before their arrival. Ultimately, all we can say is that some things happen that are beyond our control or plan. In that sense, we are at the mercy of random chance. Yet, what matters is that no matter what may occur, we have the capacity to remain steadfastly present through their dizzying arc, even to follow it and sometimes find a pot of gold at its end. None of us can say with certainty how much of our life is in our control and how much is beyond it.

The Bible also comments on chance: "The race is not to the swift, nor the battle to the strong, nor bread to the wise, nor riches to the intelligent, nor favor to the skillful; but time and chance happen to them all" (Eccl 9:11). We see in this passage that, in its relation to us, chance corresponds to grace. Both happen irrespective of our plans, our wishes, our merits or demerits. Our response to both can be audacious gratitude. Then we follow Friedrich Nietzsche's recommendation, *amor fati* ("the *love* of one's fate"). We can have faith that the gift of sustaining grace will not be far behind.

— ﷽ —

O God! that one might read the book of fate,
And see the revolution of the times.... (*Henry IV, Part Two,*
  Act III, Scene 1)

If only we could foresee our fate and that of the world around us.

There is nor flying hence nor tarrying here. (*Macbeth,* Act V,
  Scene 5)

There is no escape from fate nor a way to keep it at bay.

Well, I know not
What counts harsh fortune casts upon my face;
But in my bosom shall she never come,

Fate and Chance

To make my heart her vassal. (*Antony and Cleopatra*, Act II, Scene 6)

Fate may cause me harm, but it cannot rule my heart.

In the reproof of chance
Lies the true proof of men. (*Troilus and Cressida*, Act I, Scene 3)

Our human strength is in our capacity to stand up to the irrationality of fate.

What fates impose, that men must needs abide;
It boots not to resist both wind and tide. (*Henry VI, Part Two*, Act IV, Scene 3)

We have no power over fate. Note how this contradicts the passage above, revealing the ambiguity of the topic. The following passage asserts the ineluctability of fate.

Giddy Fortune's furious fickle wheel,
That goddess blind,
That stands upon the rolling restless stone. (*Henry V*, Act III, Scene 6)

Fate is fickle and blind to our behavior or merit.

Thus ready for the way of life or death,
I wait the sharpest blow. (*Pericles*, Act I, Scene 1)

When I am ready for any blow that fate can deal, then I am prepared for the worst that can happen.

But let determined things to destiny
Hold unbewailed their way. (*Antony and Cleopatra*, Act III, Scene 6)

Accept what must be without crying about it.

WHAT HAPPENS TO US

Our wills and fates do so contrary run
That our devices still are overthrown;
Our thoughts are ours, their ends none of our own. (*Hamlet*,
    Act III, Scene 2)

*We try with all our wits to be in control, but it doesn't work. We
certainly have minds to engage in planning, but the consequences are
beyond our control.*

The heavens themselves
Do strike at my injustice. (*The Winter's Tale*, Act III, Scene 2)

*Even powers beyond human reckoning are taking aim against my
unjust choices.*

Never Fortune
Did play a subtler game....
O, you heavenly charmers
What things you make of us! For what we lack
We laugh, for what we have are sorry.... (*The Two Noble
    Kinsmen*, Act V, Scene 4)

Fortune plays with opposites in our lives—humor in the face of scarcity, sorrow in the face of abundance.

But as the unthought-on accident is guilty
To what we wildly do, so we profess
Ourselves to be the slaves of chance and flies
Of every wind that blows. (*The Winter's Tale*, Act IV, Scene 4)

*As unforeseen chance brought this on, we are but flies caught in its
winds.*

Dear, look up:
Though Fortune, visible an enemy,

Fate and Chance

Should chase us with my father, power no jot
Hath she to change our loves. (*The Winter's Tale*, Act V,
    Scene 1)

Even when fate joins in with those who fight our love, they will never have enough power to cancel it.

…my mind misgives
Some consequence yet hanging in the stars
Shall bitterly begin his fearful date
With this night's revels and expire the term
Of a despised life closed in my breast
By some vile forfeit of untimely death.
But He, that hath the steerage of my course,
Direct my sail! (*Romeo and Juliet*, Act I, Scene 4)

I feel something dangerous is about to happen beginning with tonight's excitement. May God direct me to safety.

Whose solid virtue
The shot of accident nor the dart of chance
Could neither graze nor pierce…. (*Othello*, Act IV, Scene 1)

When our integrity is solidly based, it won't be thrown off course by any chance event.

…leave unexecuted
Your own renowned knowledge; quite forego
The way which promises assurance; and
Give up yourself merely to chance and hazard,
From firm security. (*Antony and Cleopatra*, Act III, Scene 7)

Surrender to the power of chance rather than take the safest path or trust what you can achieve.

77

WHAT HAPPENS TO US

To be or not to be, that is the question,
Whether 'tis nobler in the mind to suffer
The slings and arrows of outrageous fortune,
Or to take arms against a sea of troubles,
And by opposing end them? (*Hamlet*, Act III, Scene 1)

To go on existing or not is the question facing each of us. Is it bet-ter to tolerate what fate tosses our way, or to take a stand against our troubles, and thereby put an end to them? I recommend a reading of the full speech to explore the many further elements in it.

━━ ༄ ━━

We certainly have a capacity to expend effort, to move things along, and to make things happen. Yet, the consequences are beyond our grasp or power to manipulate. We may feel that we are at the mercy of fates we can't comprehend, that we are like "flies to wanton boys" (*King Lear*, Act IV, Scene 1). When something goes wrong for us, we may interpret it as karma or as our getting our just desserts. Suffering is not a punishment, only a given of life. Likewise, happiness is not a reward, only a state of mind and body that comes and goes beyond the reach of our ability to regu-late, cause, or merit.

Sometimes we sense the presence of powers we don't understand. They seem to hold our fate in their indifferent hands. We fear what those hands might do to us, how they might topple our house of cards, how they might interfere with our best laid schemes. Some-times, we see disaster approaching before it strikes. Sometimes, it hits us without warning. We may turn to a higher power, to our friends, or to a support system to ask for help. But our strength as humans is ultimately in our own ability to stand firm when fate is unkind. We can use this as our cheeky affirmation: "I let go of more than any fate can take." With such a defiant and yet stable inner strength, we can connect with whatever curveball fate may hurl our way.

Fate and Chance

To a person of faith, there is no such thing as fate, only random events that nonetheless weave themselves into a divine tapestry when we take them as opportunities for spiritual growth. Both choice and chance are the weavers of our lives. We can gladly wear their collaborative wardrobe and never be too hot or too cold. The "just right" of equanimity is then our path through happenings of any kind.

13

Our Friendly
Natural World

By "friendly," we mean a reality that is in our favor, a reality that can nurture, protect, and support us. The world of nature is fully in our favor when it provides us with food to sustain us, air so we can breathe, beauty to vitalize our aesthetic sense, and resources to construct shelter for us to relax in sunshine and provide shade. In this anxiety-provoking world, nature is likewise a source of tranquility when we are in the mountains, by a lake, or by a waterfall. We find solace in the natural world. We feel a kinship with sky and stars, even reading something about our lives in how they are arranged at our birth and throughout the chapters of our lives, if that is our belief. The stunning beauty of nature and its power to bring us a sense of safety and security can't be denied. We know there is a profound longing within us for what enchants us with its visual beauty or sings to us with its beguiling harmonies.

At the same time, we live on a planet subject to hurricanes, earthquakes, floods, fires, and viruses. Mother Earth does not defend us against her destructive lashings. She does not exempt the good people from them nor punish the evildoers with them. Likewise, there is no promise from nature that we won't fall from a mountain we climb so carefully, won't drown in waters we believed so safe, and won't be lost at sea in the storm that racked the schooner we dearly trusted.

All that nature really seems to offer us unambiguously is *hospitality*. Earth endures as our home from birth to death, even opening itself to provide our final lasting rest. We can love all its charms and learn to live with every one of its dangers. It will be up to us to hike through narrow passages and come out alive. Given that nature both helps and harms us, we can say that it is indeed friendly while always being perilous. Yet, nature is not two-faced, deceiving us. It is simply double-edged, and we are ever inching along it with joy and with caution.

— ༀ —

Our foster-nurse of nature is repose. (*King Lear*, Act IV, Scene 4)

Nature has the consolation of serenity in it.

All places that the eye of heaven visits
Are to a wise man ports and happy havens. (*Richard II*, Act I,
 Scene 3)

Any place in nature reached by the sun is a sanctuary.

Why should you want? Behold, the earth hath roots;
Within this mile break forth a hundred springs;
The oaks bear mast, the briers scarlet hips;
The bounteous housewife, nature, on each bush
Lays her full mess before you. Want! why want? (*Timon of Athens*,
 Act IV, Scene 3)

81

WHAT HAPPENS TO US

You are never in want once you partake of all that nature offers: roots, springs, nuts, berries. Nature is like a housewife who provides her family with a banquet.

Are not these woods
More free from peril than the envious court?
Here feel we but the penalty of Adam,
The seasons' difference, as the icy fang
And churlish chiding of the winter's wind,
Which, when it bites and blows upon my body,
Even till I shrink with cold, I smile and say
'This is no flattery: these are counselors
That feelingly persuade me what I am.
Sweet are the uses of adversity,
Which, like the toad, ugly and venomous,
Wears yet a precious jewel in his head;
And this our life exempt from public haunt
Finds tongues in trees, books in the running brooks,
Sermons in stones and good in everything.
I would not change it. (*As You Like It*, Act II, Scene 1)

Nature, whether in heat or cold, offers a refuge from city and internecine conflicts. In fact, when I am uncomfortable in nature, I find out more about who I really am. Now I see that hard times are valuable to my growth. I even hear helpful and inspiring messages/scriptures in trees, brooks, and stones. I find great goodness in all natural things and have no need to change them.

Come on, poor babe:
Some powerful spirit instruct the kites and ravens
To be thy nurses! Wolves and bears, they say
Casting their savageness aside have done
Like offices of pity. (*The Winter's Tale*, Act II, Scene 3)

May some gentle power teach even the wild beasts to show you pity.

Can such things be,
And overcome us like a summer's cloud,
Without our special wonder? (*Macbeth*, Act III, Scene 4)

So many things in nature arouse our awe. This passage was quoted by Ralph Waldo Emerson in "Nature."

One touch of nature makes the whole world kin. (*Troilus and Cressida*, Act III, Scene 3)

When we are sincere and authentic, we forge a sturdy link with all beings. In this passage, "nature" does not refer to the natural world. It is real human experience as opposed to that which is artificial or forced.

— ﻋ —

In Shakespeare's time, and in his usage, the word "nature" meant any of the following: the natural ungoverned world, a function, a role, natural or normal powers, human nature, personality, natural feeling, actual experience, or mortal life. Indeed, even for us today, "nature" does not refer only to the trees and other natural things in the world around us. We are natural too. Our breath is nature's way of flowing through us. When we meditatively breathe, it is nature that breathes in us and we in nature. Indeed, we can see all of nature as a metaphor, all natural things as revelations of territories in ourselves.

Shakespeare seems to surmise that nature can at times protect us. We see this especially in the charming quotation above from *A Winter's Tale* that refers to wolves and bears, fierce but somehow promising safety. Regarding the sense of a protective presence, a friendliness in nature, we hear from Ralph Waldo Emerson in his essay "Nature": "The incommunicable trees begin to persuade us to live with them....These enchantments are medicinal, they sober and heal us."

83

"Protective presence" does not mean we won't fall off a cliff if we are not careful. But it does mean that nature has given us an innate sense of how a cliff can be dangerous and an innate sense of caution to navigate danger safely. *Innate* means "natural endowment," a quality or capacity with which we are born. In the two cliffside gifts to us from Mother Nature—we can recognize danger and have a way to avoid it—she shows us exactly *how* she protects us. Nature gives us the capacities; it is then up to us to use them. Practice activates gift. This applies also to our inborn talents. We may be born with a talent for dancing, but it is activated only when we practice it.

14

The Spiritual World

Spirituality is awareness of and contact with the transcendent, the "more than" under the surface. A universal capacity of the human brain is its ability to believe in a hidden reality beyond appearances. We can cherish an experience or something as having more meaning or significance than what it may seem to have. For example, the symbol of the flag of the United States may appear to unsophisticated foreigners as a piece of rectangular cloth with stars and stripes sewed into it. But to an American, it represents more than is present in the design on the banner. It represents something that goes beyond, transcends, these external appearances.

Another example of something with meaning beyond an appearance is a "keepsake." There would be no such word if there were not a transcendent possibility in an ordinary thing. When Grandma's rosary becomes a keepsake, it takes on a special meaning to us, something unique to the rosary and to us. To the outside world, this rosary is a rosary, nothing more. But to us, it has a quality that makes it something more than beads on a chain. Its history and the hands that prayed this rosary have endowed it with a meaning that transcends the dictionary definition. Its price from a pawnbroker can't come anywhere near what value it has for us.

Spiritual consciousness recognizes that behind all appearances is a mystery that can't be fully located or defined. There is more to the world than what we see, more to us than what we know of ourselves, more to events than what we interpret, and more to life than what we could ever imagine. This is the mystery of transcendence—something beyond what can be categorized or calculated by our senses or by science.

The ultimate mystery is the Sacred Heart of the universe, the love that moves the sun and other stars. Sometimes, it shows up as a sense of new life arising when all around us, or in us, seems defunct. That is the mystery of life transcending death. We feel it as a presence sometimes, making it like an experience of something undying during a mortal moment. We can also encounter the transcendent in a kinship-closeness to the earth. Our sense of awe as we suddenly see a rainbow or gradually see a sunset is an example of contact and communion with the transcendent.

— ☾ —

There is a world elsewhere. (*Coriolanus*, Act III, Scene 3)

There is a realm of reality beyond this tangible world.

There is another comfort than this world. (*Measure for Measure*, Act V, Scene 1)

There is a source of comfort beyond what humans offer.

Is there no pity sitting in the clouds,
That sees into the bottom of my grief? (*Romeo and Juliet*, Act III, Scene 5)

The Spiritual World

Is there some power beyond this human world that sees my suffering and can help me? This question is answered in the following three passages from Hamlet.

Save me, and hover o'er me with your wings,
You heavenly guards! (*Hamlet*, Act III, Scene 4)

Guardian angels, come to my aid.

There's divinity that shapes our ends
Rough hew them as we will. (*Hamlet*, Act V, Scene 2)

A higher power than our ego shapes our life no matter how we mess it up.

There are more things in heaven and earth, Horatio,
Than are dreamt of in your philosophy. (*Hamlet*, Act I, Scene 5)

Be open to what is strange and new since there is more to reality than what we think it to be.

Now bless thyself: thou meetest with things dying, I with things
   newborn. (*The Winter's Tale*, Act III, Scene 3)

Now cross your heart: as you met with death, I met with birth.

And take upon us the mystery of things,
As if we were God's spies. (*King Lear*, Act V, Scene 3)

There is a mystery in all beings and phenomena, more than we ever guessed was there.

This is as strange a maze as e'er men trod
And there is in this business more than nature

WHAT HAPPENS TO US

Was ever conduct of: some oracle
Must rectify our knowledge. (*The Tempest*, Act V, Scene 1)

We need help from a transcendent wisdom to help us out of this bewildering perplexity.

…soft stillness and the night
Become the touches of sweet harmony….
Such harmony is in immortal souls,
But whilst this muddy vesture of decay
Doth grossly close it in, we cannot hear it. (*Merchant of Venice*,
    Act V, Scene 1)

The harmony of the universe is the harmony of wholeness within us. We can't hear it when we are caught up in materiality or in ego-driven pursuits that deafens our souls.

Go with me, like good angels, to my end;
And, as the long divorce of steel falls on me,
Make of your prayers one sweet sacrifice,
And lift my soul to heaven. (*Henry VIII*, Act II, Scene 1)

Accompany me like angels and, as my end comes, lift me to heaven.

After death our spirits shall be led
To those that love eternally. (*The Two Noble Kinsmen*, Act II,
    Scene 2)

We shall be reunited after death with those who loved us and with all those who have ever loved.

— ℯℓℯ —

We touch things with our hands, but our heart can feel into the intangible. This gives us a kinship with the depth dimension in the universe, more that eyes like ours can see. We feel a harmonizing with rhythms that go beyond sound and sight. It feels enduring, undeniably real, something that survives and defies death. When we go beyond the merely material in our vision, go beyond grasping and consuming in our choices, we come upon this spiritual world. It is all aglow but only to those who keep peering into it and are committed to its call to be one with it.

An underlying spiritual reality in all that is and in all that happens does not let us down, even in "these most brisk and giddy-paced times" (*Twelfth Night*, Act II, Scene 4). What is it that does not let us down? We can call it God, higher power, the life force of the universe. This is the ultimate transcendent reality, the More behind all that is, the More that is the All. We might also describe it as I have over the years:

Something,
We know not what,
Is always and everywhere
lovingly at work,
we know not how,
to make the world more than it is now
to make us more than we are yet.
That Something is what we call:
a Higher Power,
the life force of the universe,
our own true nature,
already and always what makes us one.

15

The Journey to Wholeness

Wholeness refers to completion not perfection. We keep feeling disappointed in ourselves when we try to do everything exactly as it *should* be done. Trusting that there is a wholeness already and always richly in us makes us more secure about simply being ourselves. Our journey is not technically to wholeness. Our journey is to a recovery and revelation of it.

As humans, we aren't like the tiger who gets every instinct right. We aren't like the mountain that always stands firm. We aren't like the water that always finds a way to flow. We find ourselves sometimes frozen or dammed. Wholeness is a capacity that awaits incarnation, not a guarantee that we will get it all right.

We can trust, however, that, regardless of how we display ourselves in the daily grind, our underlying design is whole and reliable. Then our own inner life becomes a home to go from as well as a refuge to which we can return.

Indeed, our inner life is animated by a life-giving and life-affirming spirit that does not desert us no matter what may happen or how we act. This God-life in us—a trinity of love, wisdom, and healing power—is our very essence, untainted by our past choices or present behavior. Our spiritual practices are aimed at activating this enlightened identity in us. This happens through a series of existential choices, here and now actions that manifest in time, our lifetime, the timeless love, wisdom, and healing power that is in us, and that is us. Our journey to wholeness is to find it by going in and coming out to reveal it.

— ﷽ —

When we are born, we cry that we have come to this stage of
     fools. (*King Lear*, Act IV, Scene 6)

Our first cry was a recognition that we were born into a world of fools.

I have a journey, sir, shortly to go.
My master calls me; I must not say no. (*King Lear*, Act V,
     Scene 3)

I feel called to a journey to Yes. This is the spiritual journey.

Lear: You see how this world goes.
Gloucester: I see it feelingly. (*King Lear*, Act IV, Scene 6)

I am touched by the world and events.

A true devoted pilgrim is not weary
To measure kingdoms with his feeble steps. (*Two Gentlemen of
     Verona*, Act II, Scene 7)

When we are truly committed to the human journey, we don't get discouraged by how feebly we walk.

Happily I have arrived at the last

WHAT HAPPENS TO US

Unto the wished haven of my bliss. (*The Taming of the Shrew*, Act V, Scene 1)

Now I am at the place that I had always wished I would find.

In nature's infinite book of secrecy
A little I can read. (*Antony and Cleopatra*, Act I, Scene 2)

I am aware of the infinite mystery that is human nature and can even make out some of it.

What a piece of work is a man! How noble in reason!
How infinite in faculty! In form and moving how
Express and admirable! In action how like an angel
In apprehension how like a god! The beauty of the world,
The paragon of animals. (*Hamlet*, Act II, Scene 2)

We humans have a noble nature. We have capacities without limit. We move like angels. Our ability to understand is a divine grace. We stand out in beauty, a model for all other earthly beings.

Our stars must glister with new fire or be
Today extinct. (*The Two Noble Kinsmen*, Act V, Scene 1)

When we find new enthusiasms and are on fire with new energy, we are truly and beautifully alive. Without such animation we die.

— ⚜ —

Wholeness is being wholly excited by the energies every-where around us, letting them light a fire in our hearts and under our feet.

Wholeness manifests itself when we are wholly enunciating a yes to the way things are and wholly at work to make things better.

92

Wholeness means being wholly moved by all that happens to the world and all its beings.

Wholeness is being wholly committed to a life of compassion toward those who suffer, including ourselves.

Wholeness is letting go of hankering for the green grass on the other side of our own garden. In wholeness, there are no more sides in any sense of that word.

Wholeness is being wholly dedicated to our journey to full consciousness no matter how confused our minds may be.

Wholeness is in us by the fact of our humanness. When we judge ourselves for being inadequate, the spiritual goal is to acknowledge that inadequacy as a given of life. Our unconditional yes to that leads us to do what it takes to improve our daily life skills.

Wholeness is having within us the Sacred Heart of the universe, what makes everything evolve and revolve in joy and creativity. The center of this Heart is everywhere, its circumference nowhere. To be whole is thus to be a participant in infinity and an heir of eternity.

Wholeness has happened when we no longer believe we have come from nothing and are going back to nothing. Wholeness happens when we know we have come from everything and are going back to everything.

Wholeness calls us to become in action what we are in fact.

16

Death

We are born; we live out our lifetime; we die.
When any of this will happen and how long our time
here will last is not in our hands.

All we know is that our time is limited.

We are here to become ourselves in the time we have.

In spiritual consciousness, we want to do all the good we can in
the time remaining to us.

We don't forget we will die; we don't bring it on ourselves; we
don't impose it on others.

We accept the fact of an ending of life on this plane.

At the same time, we may trust or believe that a new life awaits
us hereafter.

That gives us comfort and may, on the one hand, motivate us
to act with virtue and love in all our dealings.

We may, on the other hand, believe that death is the end
indeed.

Then we want to use every minute of this precious life to be all
that we are, all that every human is: limited and individual vessels
as well as channels of a deathless and universal love.

Death

When we open to that calling, death is not an end but a fulfill-ment.

— ꩜ —

But here must end the story of my life. (*The Comedy of Errors*,
   Act I, Scene 1)

A time to die is inevitable.

I must yield my body to the earth....
Thus yields the cedar to the axe's edge,
Whose arms gave shelter to the princely eagle,
Under whose shade the rampling lion slept.... (*Henry VI*,
   Part Three, Act V, Scene 2)

*I now turn my body and life over to the earth the same way the cedar
tree yields to the axe even though it was once a shelter for the eagle and
gave shade to a wandering lion.*

This world's a city full of straying streets,
And death's the market-place where each one meets. (*The Two
   Noble Kinsmen*, Act I, Scene 5)

Our world is full of aimless paths, and they all intersect with death.

You ever–gentle gods, take my breath from me;
Let not my worser spirit tempt me again
To die before you please. (*King Lear*, Act IV, Scene 6)

*May God be the arbiter of how long I live. I don't want to go by
suicide.*

I do find it cowardly and vile,
For fear of what might fall, so to prevent

WHAT HAPPENS TO US

The time of life: arming myself with patience
To stay the providence of some high powers
That govern us below. (*Julius Caesar*, Act V, Scene 1)

*I surrender in patience to the will of the gods regarding my lifeline.
It would be cowardly to do myself in so I can avoid pain in the future.*

…'tis too horrible.
The weariest and most loathed worldly life
That age, ache, penury and imprisonment
Can lay on nature is a paradise
To what we fear of death. (*Measure for Measure*, Act III,
    Scene 1)

*No matter how bad our life predicaments are, they cannot compare
to the fear of death and its aftermath.*

I have immortal longings in me. (*Antony and Cleopatra*, Act V,
    Scene 2)

I am ready to die and enter eternity.

In peace and honor rest you here, my sons;
Rome's readiest champions, repose you here in rest,
Secure from worldly chances and mishaps!
Here lurks no treason, here no envy swells,
Here grow no damned grudges; here are no storms,
No noise, but silence and eternal sleep:
In peace and honor rest you here, my sons! (*Titus Andronicus*,
    Act I, Scene 1)

*You can rest in peace, my sons. Here you are beyond the reach of
chance, betrayal, envy, grudges, storms, and discord. Now there is only
silence, honor, and eternal rest for you.*

Death

Yet this my comfort: when your words are done,
My woes end likewise with the evening sun. (*The Comedy of
    Errors*, Act I, Scene 1)

*I am condemned to die, but at least I have this comfort: when your
verdict is pronounced, my troubles will also end—at sundown, that is,
at the end.*

More are men's ends mark'd than their lives before:
The setting sun, and music at the close,
As the last taste of sweets, is sweetest last,
Writ in remembrance more than things long past. (*Richard II*,
    Act II, Scene 1)

*People notice our death more than our lifetime. An ending is sweeter
somehow than a memory of what is past.*

Even through the hollow eyes of death
I spy life peering. (*Richard II*, Act II, Scene 1)

Even in death there is life.

Men must endure
Their going hence, even as their coming hither.
Ripeness is all. (*King Lear*, Act V, Scene 2)

*We must accept death and endings just as we accept birth and begin-
nings. Being ready is all that matters.*

— ☾ —

That death awaits all of us follows from the fact that everything
is impermanent. It is a given that everything changes and that
everything ends. This applies to our interests, our relationships, our
health, our timeline here on planet earth. It is a spiritual practice,

a spiritual victory, to embrace our death as we might have welcomed our birth. Beginnings, middles, and endings can become guests to whom we provide equal hospitality.

The word "ripeness" in the final quotation above refers to readiness. We remain at the ready throughout life for the continuous parade of changes that will pass before us. What happens does not matter as much as how courageously and graciously we face it and move through it. This kind of readiness becomes an inner resource. We notice we can handle what comes our way with more confidence. We are not in control but fully empowered. When who we are is defined as being "in control," we will fear death, the ultimate experience of not being in control.

There are two realities we often deny: one is grief; the other is death. We hide from our sadness at an ending of something in our lives. We hide from our acknowledgment of our death, the ending of our own life. Our society participates in this twofold denial. We certainly all know we will die, but we refuse to acknowledge it fully, that is, more than in words. Some of us don't even prepare for it. Yet our bodies know when our time has come; our bodies will even know how to die.

Our belief in an afterlife is a way to prevent death from having the final word. We hope we can live on in a new way. St. Thérèse believed in an afterlife and promised that she would spend her time in heaven doing good on earth. That possibility of helping our fellow humans after we die makes belief in the afterlife not a hope for ongoing self-preservation but a wondrous grace. In mature spiritual consciousness, the chance to go on being of service after death makes an afterlife a spiritual practice.

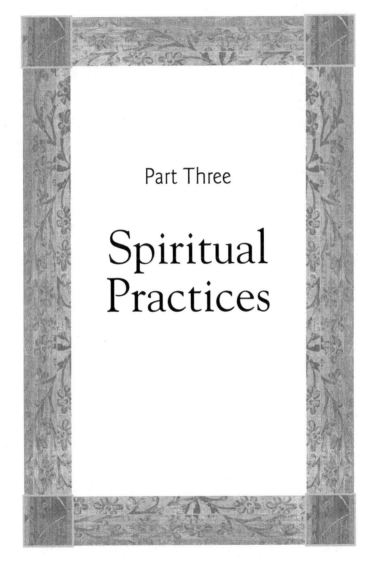

Part Three

Spiritual
Practices

17

Showing and Being Compassion

In these next nine chapters, we present specific spiritual practices based on recommendations by Shakespeare, or perhaps we can now call him the Abbot of the Earth Monastery of the Brothers and Sisters of Humanness.

Our first spiritual practice is compassion. In true compassion, we do more than simply see someone's suffering sympathetically. This may be a one-up dualism that opposes authentic spiritual practice. In spiritually aware compassion, we see others as peers, fellow sufferers. We see with caring empathy; we are in the other's shoes. This lifts compassion from being merely an observing of those in pain. To empathize combines feeling with a sense of full connection to the other. Thus, compassion is a form of intimacy, a deep contact, something we feel in our body and show in bodily ways.

In true compassion our response is not based on how tugged we are by a particular person's pitiable plight. Spiritual compassion is universal and unconditional. We feel compassion for any and every form of suffering. As an example, we are compassionate toward victims and persecutors alike, though we show our compassion to each of them in different ways. We show compassion for the victims of abuse by leaning into their condition and finding ways to be of service, the style of the good Samaritan. We show compassion for the perpetrator of abuse by supporting programs that combine restorative justice and the opportunity for therapy, the style of a wise judge.

Furthermore, our compassion for the downtrodden in society becomes truly real when we attempt to heal the *causes* of their suffering. This working for justice is the complement of a compassionate feeling. We dedicate ourselves to address the issues in society that have led to the suffering. We work to accomplish the political changes that will make a difference. This is engaged compassion, the full spectrum of compassion that engages both our hearts and our hands.

— ༄ —

O, I have suffered
With those that I saw suffer! (*The Tempest*, Act I, Scene 2)

The suffering that I see in others I feel in myself.

Take physic, Pomp;
Expose thyself to feel what wretches feel. (*King Lear*, Act III,
    Scene 4)

Learn from a high position to feel compassion for those on lower rungs of the ladder.

Now I see the mystery of your loneliness. (*All's Well that Ends
    Well*, Act I, Scene 3)

Now I can have empathy for your feeling of isolation.

Showing and Being Compassion

My pity hath been balm to heal their wounds,
My mildness hath allayed their swelling griefs.... (*Henry VI,
    Part Three*, Act V, Scene 8)

My compassion has healed injuries; my kindness has allayed grief.

A most poor man, made tame to fortune's blows,
Who by the art of known and feeling sorrows
Am pregnant to good pity. (*King Lear*, Act IV, Scene 6)

*My own bad luck has made me more gentle, and my sufferings have
made me more compassionate.*

...they find a kind of ease,
Bearing their own misfortunes on the back
Of such as have before endured the like. (*Richard II*, Act V,
    Scene 5)

*We can find comfort knowing that all humans suffer in similar ways.
There is a healing power in this realization.*

None can be called deformed but the unkind. (*Twelfth Night*,
    Act III, Scene 4)

*Unkindness deforms our true nature, which is intrinsically good.
In compassion, we act kindly toward all beings, not only toward those
who are appealing.*

Cassius to his friend Brutus:
Have not you love enough to bear with me,
When that rash humor which my mother gave me
Makes me forgetful? (*Julius Caesar*, Act IV, Scene 3)

*I ask you to show your love to me by making allowances for the
aggressive nature I inherited from my mother.*

SPIRITUAL PRACTICES

A friendly eye could never see such faults. (*Julius Caesar*, Act IV,
  Scene 3)

If you really love me, you will not judge me by my defects.

Forbear to judge, for we are sinners all.
Close up his eyes, and draw the curtain close;
And let us all to meditation. (*Henry VI, Part Two*, Act III,
  Scene 3)

Our spiritual practices help us not to judge or censure others.

If you now beheld them, your affections
Would become tender. (*The Tempest*, Act V, Scene 1)

*If you saw others as they really are, your loving-kindness would
open to them.*

Sweet mercy is nobility's true badge. (*Titus Andronicus*, Act I,
  Scene 1)

*The more advanced we are, the higher our rank, the more compas-
sionate we become.*

The quality of mercy is not strained.
It droppeth as the gentle rain from heaven
Upon the place beneath. It is twice blest:
It blesseth him that gives and him that takes.
'Tis mightiest in the mightiest; it becomes
The thronèd monarch better than his crown.
His scepter shows the force of temporal power,
The attribute to awe and majesty
Wherein doth sit the dread and fear of kings;
But mercy is above this sceptered sway.
It is enthronèd in the hearts of kings;

Showing and Being Compassion

It is an attribute to God Himself;
And earthly power doth then show likest God's
When mercy seasons justice. (*Merchant of Venice*, Act IV,
Scene 1)

Nothing can hold back our compassion. It flows out like the rain reaching both those who give and those who receive. It shows itself more strongly in those who are strongest. It is greater than royal power, more powerful than royal authority. It is a heart quality, like the compassion in the heart of God. So, our acting with justice is godlike when we combine it with mercy.

— ☪ —

An essential feature of love is to feel compassion for the suffering of others. We feel moved to establish and maintain a caring connection with those in pain, be it physical, emotional, or spiritual. The suffering may come from natural causes or the givens of life, for instance, losses, accidents, or illness. If we find ourselves judging others for their suffering, our practice is to transform judgment into compassion.

In mature spiritual consciousness, we become especially sensitive specifically toward those who suffer because of the harm others do to them. Likewise, when we grow in compassion, we notice we become committed not to hurt others ourselves. Non-harming is an automatic result of feeling compassion.

The call of love is to show active engaged compassion, that is, expressed in deed not only in word, as we noted above. We feel moved by suffering and then dedicate ourselves to end the causes of suffering, an impossible feat but we are trusting a power beyond our ego to assist us. From a spiritual perspective, even a small change for the better is the equivalent of complete success.

In spiritual maturity, our compassion also becomes universal in its extent. It is not only shown to those we love but to anyone who crosses our path. In Christianity, Christ is a model of

105

engaged compassion since he responded so readily to the needs of others. In Buddhism, compassion results from the wisdom that sees no distinction, no separateness anywhere, not even between one person and another. This is what was referred to in the introduction to this section as compassion being shown to victim and persecutor alike. Instead of division, both in Christian and Buddhist teaching, we see union, oneness. When we act with compassion, this union becomes communion, and only one heart beats in all of us.

Mercy triumphs over judgment.

—James 2:13

18

A Life of Virtue and Integrity

Virtue refers to moral rectitude shown in commendable behavior, that is, aligning ourselves to standards of goodness and the social contract.

Integrity refers to a commitment to act in upright ways:

* to be honest in all our dealings,
* to keep our agreements, and
* to show decency of character in our behavior and attitudes toward others.

A major feature of being truly human is to embrace virtue and integrity as commitments that will govern all that we say and do. We want to be in the world as people who

* follow the golden rule,
* sincerely care about others, and
* show respect to all beings regardless of their status.

SPIRITUAL PRACTICES

We act in accord with standards that are based on integrity regardless of whether others do the same.

We show virtue and integrity because they have become who we are, no reward needed or expected.

Our commitment to personal integrity is matched by our loving-kindness toward others.

These commitments have become habitual because we have not given up on practicing them.

They have become sources of healthy pride in us and resources of service to others.

— ॐ —

From lowest place when virtuous things proceed,
The place is dignified by the doer's deed. (*All's Well that Ends
   Well*, Act II, Scene 3)

No matter how low one's station, it is elevated by a virtuous deed.

Virtue is bold and goodness never fearful. (*Measure for Measure*,
   Act III, Scene 1)

When we show goodness, we become courageous, and our fear vanishes.

He was ever precise in promise-keeping. (*Measure for Measure*,
   Act I, Scene 2)

He keeps his agreements diligently.

Thy promises are like Adonis' gardens
That one day bloomed and fruitful were the next. (*Henry VI, Part
   One*, Act I, Scene 6)

A Life of Virtue and Integrity

Your promises can be trusted to bear fruit.

His words are bonds, his oaths are oracles,
His love sincere, his thoughts immaculate,
His tears pure messengers sent from his heart,
His heart as far from fraud as heaven from earth. (*Two Gentlemen
   of Verona*, Act II, Scene 7)

*You can trust what he says and swears. He is pure-minded. His
griefs are sincere. He speaks and acts from the heart.*

This fellow's of exceeding honesty,
And knows all qualities, with a learned spirit,
Of human dealings. (*Othello*, Act III, Scene 3)

*Here is a person who understands human nature and how we
interact.*

No legacy is so rich as honesty. (*All's Well that Ends Well*, Act III,
   Scene 5)

The best bequest is truthfulness.

His life was gentle, and the elements
So mix'd in him that Nature might stand up
And say to all the world "This was a man!" (*Julius Caesar*, Act V,
   Scene 5)

*His loving-kindness showed him to be a truly humane person and an
exemplar of humanness.*

That monster, custom, who all sense doth eat,
Of habits devil, is angel yet in this,

SPIRITUAL PRACTICES

That to the use of actions fair and good,
He likewise gives a frock or livery,
That aptly is put on. (*Hamlet*, Act III, Scene 4)

Habit can be a terrible thing when it means becoming used to doing what is evil without feeling bad about it. But habit can also be a good thing, especially when being good also becomes habitual. Here is a quotation that supports the positive dimension: "For use almost can change the stamp of nature." (*Hamlet*, Act III, Scene 4)

Now bid me run,
And I will strive with things impossible;
Yea, get the better of them. (*Julius Caesar*, Act II, Scene 1)

Urge me on, and I will succeed.

Give me a staff of honor for mine age,
But not a scepter to control the world. (*Titus Andronicus*, Act I, Scene 1)

I want to be honored for my mature wisdom not for my being in control. (Give me a staff to honor my wisdom but don't offer me a scepter with which to dominate the world.)

How far that little candle throws his beams!
So shines a good deed in a naughty world. (*The Merchant of Venice*, Act V, Scene 1)

An act of goodness is a light to the world. This is the first quotation from Shakespeare that I saved. It happened in high school English class when I was fourteen.

A Life of Virtue and Integrity

Our love is what makes us human. No matter how badly situations play out, no matter how harsh people become, we can act with standards of loving-kindness and integrity. We can move toward the good and that even becomes our source of safety and security. This is because our goodness, shown in action, helps us esteem and trust ourselves as we notice our fears dissolving. *When all that matters is our dedication to what is right and good, there is nothing left to fear.*

In all of this, we may need help from others. They encourage us to follow our standards faithfully; they nudge us when we don't follow them. These paraphrased words from Dr. Martin Luther King Jr. last sermon say it all:

> Every now and again, I think of dying, and I wonder how I will be remembered. I hope my eulogist won't mention my Nobel Peace Prize, my education, my other awards....I want to be remembered as one who tried to love somebody. Let him say: Martin Luther King tried to feed the hungry, to clothe the naked, to visit the imprisoned....I won't have any money to leave behind. I won't have the fine and luxurious things of life to leave behind. All I leave behind is a committed life. Jesus, I don't want to be on your right or left side because of fame but because of love."*

This can become our daily affirmation:

May I show all the love I have
In any way I can, wherever I may be,
Today and all the time,
To everyone—including me—
Since love is what we really are

---

* Adapted from Martin Luther King, Jr., "The Drum Major Instinct" sermon at Ebenezer Baptist Church at Atlanta, Georgia, February 4, 1968.

And what we're here to share.
Now nothing matters to me more
Or gives me greater joy.
May all our world become
One Sacred Heart of love.

19

Sharing Our Gifts

In the twelfth and last step toward recovery in the Alcoholics Anonymous program we hear, "Having had a spiritual awakening as a result of these steps, we tried to carry this message to [other] alcoholics...." A spiritual awakening turns into a gift to others not only a benefit for the person taking the steps. When our spiritual journey takes us to any height, we notice that we automatically want to share the riches we have found. We don't keep our talents, gifts, realizations, advances, or prized growth experiences to ourselves. Something in us feels drawn to spread the news, share the good feelings, and tell and bring to others the gifts we have been given.

Aristotle observed that goodness always wants to share, "diffuse" itself. It is of the very nature of goodness and love to spread itself around. Paradoxically, this sharing does not diminish us but only expand us. There is always *more* goodness and love in us, more than we might ever guess. As Juliet says, "The more I give to thee the more I have for both are infinite" (*Romeo and Juliet*, Act II, Scene 2). We never have to fear that love will disappear, only that we might not trust its abundance enough.

SPIRITUAL PRACTICES

Thus, our progress and awakenings come to fruition precisely in our sharing of them. Our spiritual commitment is ultimately to help all beings find the enlightened way that we have excitedly discovered, the path that we have joyously walked, and the doorway that we have daringly opened into the divine. This commitment is not something we make happen; it is grace that moves us to altruism, a grace available to all of us. Our spiritual practice is to trust that grace and then to let it happen.

—— ༄ ——

The gift doth stretch itself as 'tis received,
And is enough for both. (*All's Well that Ends Well*, Act II, Scene 1)

When we share our gift, it expands so that all benefit.

Good fellows all,
The latest of my wealth I'll share amongst you. (*Timon of Athens*, Act IV, Scene 2)

In camaraderie I share my riches with all of you.

What is yours to bestow is not yours to reserve. (*Twelfth Night*, Act I, Scene 5)

You were given gifts and graces so that you could share them.

Heaven doth with us as we with torches do,
Not light them for themselves; for if our virtues
Did not go forth of us, 'twere all alike
As if we had them not. (*Measure for Measure*, Act I, Scene 1)

We were meant to show our light to the world, not merely shine it on ourselves. This is true of virtue. If it is not used to light the way for others, it may as well not exist.

114

Sure, he that made us with such large discourse,
Looking before and after, gave us not
That capability and god-like reason
To fust in us unused. (*Hamlet*, Act IV, Scene 4)

We are here to put our gifts to good use, not let them become moldy.

A largess universal, like the sun,
His liberal eye doth give to everyone. (*Henry V*, Act IV, Prologue)

His generosity and openness extend to all.

— ☙ —

As we have noted so far, our inborn gifts and talents came with a calling that we use them not only for ourselves but for others. This follows from being a member of the human family, engaged in a collaborative project, one requiring that we help one another, each according to his or her own set of endowments and skills. Why is there light in us unless it is meant to shine on those waiting for the light in the dim corners of our dark world? One of the mottos of the Dominican order is "to contemplate and to give to others the fruits of contemplation." This summarizes our calling to bring to others what we have found and benefited from.

The obstacles to self-giving are listed in Buddhism as the three poisonings of enlightenment: greed, hate, and ignorance. All three constrict us so we are disabled from fulfilling our spiritual life purpose to share our gifts:

- In *greed*, we hold onto what we find and have, refusing to be generous, refusing to apportion our abundance.
- In *hate*, we want others to fail and trip rather than give them a leg up. We live in the grip of prejudice and exclusion. We hold rancor against those who are different from us.

* In *ignorance* we imagine we are all separate rather than one human family. Then the world seems to be our own oyster while none of its pearls can ever find their way out of our own permanently locked jewelry box.

Our spiritual practice is to bestow what we have on others as so many others have bestowed what they have had on us. The life of goodness and happiness is an endless chain of receiving and giving. Graces come so they can go.

> *Love is the only thing you get more of*
> *by giving it away.*
>
> —Antoine de Saint-Exupéry, *The Little Prince*

20

Restoring Ourselves through Suffering

Suffering can help us. It is redemptive when we move through it with courage rather than be frozen in fear by its wallop. We do this without resentment that suffering has happened to us. We then grow because of what we have lived through. This does not mean that we tolerate abuse. Rather, we accept the natural pain that can result from the painful givens of life and disturbing events that come our way. For example: We are betrayed in a relationship—something that can happen to anyone. We feel hurt and a keen grief. With spiritual consciousness, we choose not to act on our natural inclination, retaliation. We open ourselves to the unwelcome reality, find a way through its confounding maze, and move on in life.

In this spiritual practice, our suffering has made us stronger, evoking our courage as well as our loving-kindness. We have broadened our capacity to love, ironically and precisely because someone was unloving toward us. This is an example of how suffering becomes redemptive—how it can increase our spiritual maturity and widen our embrace of others. It's certainly a tall order, but we can be sure that graces will come our way so that we will be ready to fulfill it.

"Redemption" in Latin refers to "buying back." We use it that way now when we say we are redeeming a ticket. Thus, redemption means restoring to us what is rightfully ours. Our very being has always been full of courage and loving-kindness, and we have bought them back from the world of pain—with a commitment never to inflict pain on others.

— ☙ —

Be cheerful; wipe thine eyes
Some falls are means the happier to arise. (*Cymbeline*, Act IV,
    Scene 2)

Don't be sad. Some of our faults and mistakes help us rise higher than we were before.

This music crept by me upon the waters,
Allaying both their fury and my passion
With its sweet air…. (*The Tempest*, Act II, Scene 2)

I got in touch with harmonies that freed both nature and me from aggression and craving.

My desolation does begin to make a better life. (*Antony and
    Cleopatra*, Act V, Scene 2)

My sufferings are beginning to promise relief.

Our remedies oft in ourselves do lie
Which we ascribe to heaven: the fated sky
Gives us free scope, only doth backward pull
Our slow designs when we ourselves are dull. (*All's Well that Ends
    Well*, Act I, Scene 1)

Restoring Ourselves through Suffering

We can often trust our self-healing powers rather than think they require help from beyond us in order to work. In fact, fate gives us free rein and we only fall back when we are lazy or too slow. The following quotation offers another perspective: "Men at some time are masters of their fates: / The fault, dear Brutus, is not in our stars, / But in ourselves, that we are underlings (*Julius Caesar*, Act I, Scene 2).

People can experience mastery in their lives. If you and I are failing, it is not based on fate but on our own inadequacy—and our having lower ranks than someone else [Caesar].

If ever you have spent time worse ere now;
If never, yet that Time himself doth say
He wishes earnestly you never may. (*A Winter's Tale*, Act IV,
    Scene 1)

We can let go of regret about the past for time itself approves of letting go, since it helps it happen.

Macbeth: Canst thou not minister to a mind diseased,
Pluck from the memory a rooted sorrow,
Raze out the written troubles of the brain,
And with some sweet oblivious antidote
Cleanse the stuffed bosom of that perilous stuff,
Which weighs upon the heart?
Doctor: Therein the patient
Must minister to himself. (*Macbeth*, Act V, Scene 3)

Sometimes, healing depends only on ourselves.

'Tis good for men to love their present pains
Upon example: so the spirit is eased. (*Henry V*, Act IV, Scene 1)

SPIRITUAL PRACTICES

It is good for us to accept our present suffering in imitation of others who do so. Then we find contentment and serenity.

Oft expectation fails, and most oft there
Where most it promises; and oft it hits
Where hope is coldest, and despair most fits. (*All's Well that Ends
    Well*, Act II, Scene 1)

We often experience disappointment when what we had hoped for did not work out. But success can also happen when we thought it impossible.

Naught's had, all's spent
When our desire is got without content. (*Macbeth*, Act III,
    Scene 2)

Having what we wanted but not being satisfied with it, leaves us feeling as if we have nothing after all.

$$— \text{☙} —$$

Not only our suffering but our errors and regrets can turn into what is useful to our growth. We might find ourselves now more evolved because of how far we fell before. For instance, an alcoholic who hits bottom but then recovers in a program feels better off because of all the inner healing that happens in the recovery experience.

When we suffer and survive our suffering we build and access inner resources of healing—the components of wholeness in each of us. We could only have found them in our own experiences, usually the painful ones helping the most. It is a paradox of human existence that without pain and grief there is no deepening of our sense of ourselves and our capacities. This is also an instance of how the errors we have committed during our lives can be catalysts to a better life in the present. When we hang out with regret for the mistakes we have made and the errors we have repeated, we miss out on the possibility of a wonderful alchemy: to transform what seems worthless into what has abundant value and restorative power. We hear of this in comforting images from a modern poet:

> Last night as I was sleeping,
> I dreamt—marvelous error!—
> that I had a beehive
> here inside my heart.
> And the golden bees
> were making white combs
> and sweet honey
> from my old failures. (Antonio Machado, "Last Night as I was Sleeping")

21

From Revenge to Reconciliation

Most of us believe that we can adjust the scales of injustice by getting back at the one who harmed us. We imagine that revenge or rage will salve our grief so that we won't have to feel it so acutely. Retaliation is a primitive method of avoiding the vulnerability that we feel when we are hurt, treated unfairly, disappointed, or betrayed.

Our spiritual practice and our psychological work present a three-step alternative:

- We let ourselves fully experience our grief. This includes sadness about what happened, anger at the one who made it happen, and fear we will not survive it.
- We say "Ouch!" literally or in whatever way communicates to the other the painful impact of the other person's behavior on us. We do this assertively but not aggressively.

- We offer to open a dialogue so reconciliation can happen. If the offender is unwilling to join us in this, we let go with loving-kindness and move on with our own life.

We can choose to take these steps rather than immediately jump to revenge. We can commit ourselves today to this spiritual practice in preparation for the next time an injustice is inflicted upon us.

In Latin, the word *retaliation* means to do the same to another as was done to us. It is the opposite of the golden rule. The yen for revenge makes us mean-spirited, out for blood, cruel. Our three-step program is a nonviolent alternative.

The most beautiful capacity in us is forgiveness. It can open in us as we let go of the need for retaliation. Forgiveness does not mean excusing abuse. It is a letting go of ill will, blame, resentment, and the need to retaliate. This comes about after we feel and show our grief and state our "Ouch!" Forgiveness is a grace that comes to us provided our ego does not get in our way.

My honour'd lady,
I have forgiven and forgotten all;
Though my revenges were high bent upon him,
And watch'd the time to shoot. (*All's Well that Ends Well*, Act V, Scene 3)

I forgive and forget his offenses, letting go of my plan to retaliate.

Stay thy revengeful hand; thou hast no cause to fear. (*Richard II*, Act V, Scene 3)

SPIRITUAL PRACTICES

Fear is the ultimate motive for revenge. When we let go of the need to retaliate, we free ourselves from fear.

It is a quarrel most unnatural
To be revenged on him that loveth you. (*Richard III*, Act I,
    Scene 2)

To take revenge on someone who loves you does not fit with true love.

…he did but see
The flatness of my misery, yet with eyes
Of pity, not revenge! (*A Winter's Tale*, Act III, Scene 2)

In seeing my pain, he chose to show compassion rather than to retaliate.

All have not offended;
For those that were, it is not square to take
On those that are, revenges: crimes, like lands,
Are not inherited. Then, dear countryman,
Bring in thy ranks, but leave without thy rage. (*Timon of Athens*,
    Act V, Scene 4)

Let go of rage and the need to exact revenge.

Had all his hairs been lives, my great revenge
Had stomach for them all. (*Othello*, Act V, Scene 2)

I am dead set on revenge in every cell of my body.

Though with their high wrongs I am struck to the quick,
Yet with my nobler reason against my fury
Do I take part: the rarer action is
In virtue than in vengeance: they being penitent,

From Revenge to Reconciliation

The sole drift of my purpose doth extend
Not a frown further. (*The Tempest*, Act V, Scene 1)

Even though I have been hurt by how others acted toward me and am angry at them, I will access my healthy noble sentiments. It is rarer to act with kindness and forgiveness than with vengeance. Likewise, when others are sorry for what they have done, my desire to punish them vanishes.

...kindness, nobler ever than revenge.... (*As You Like It*, Act IV, Scene 3)

Compassion is the virtue that releases us from the will to retaliate.

— ـﻠـ —

The desire for vengeance takes over our whole being, stressing our bodies, setting destructive fire to our soul. When we have embraced the alternative practice of loving-kindness, we look for ways to make up with those who have hurt us rather than hurt them back. We also let go even of wanting someone to "what's coming to him." Instead, we hope he finds a path to growth in wisdom and love.

We no longer hope that "what goes around comes around." We hope that what happens to all of us is a turnaround from hurting or harming one another to treating one another with loving-kindness. This is an example of a conversion from hate to love, from fear to friendship, from heartless, mindless street mentality to the heart of Christ or mind of Buddha.

That attitude leads to a yearning for reconciliation. We let go of the primitive need to punish, the cave people's legacy in us. The spiritually aware style comes to us from the legacy of evolved humans. Both capacities are in us. It is up to us to choose our domicile, the cave of fear and hate or the "open sesame" of a full and loving humanity.

SPIRITUAL PRACTICES

We might say, metaphorically, that throughout our lives we are accompanied by a wolf and a dog. The wolf of hate and revenge slinks along on one side while the friendly dog of love and reconciliation accompanies us on the other. We feed the wolf by acting with vengeful hate. We feed the dog by acting with forgiving love. The strength of each of them grows in accord with how much we feed them. Both remain with us for a lifetime, but it is up to us which one will grow more robustly.

22

Making Amends

What is our path to reconciliation and personal transformation when we offend others? The essence of restorative justice is to make amends for our offences and thereby rejoin the human community. When we have hurt others, we acknowledge it and ask forgiveness. Hamlet says to Laertes, "I have shot my arrow o'er the house and hurt my brother" (*Hamlet*, Act V, Scene 2). Healthy humans don't knowingly hurt others. Likewise, healthy humans never hate, that is, hold ill will, rage, and have an insatiable need to retaliate. The making of amends refers to righting the scales of justice that have been thrown off-center by our untoward actions. When we are healthy, psychologically and spiritually, we *want* to do this.

Here is the full program of making up for how we have wronged others:

- We admit that what we did was wrong or offensive.
- We show we are sorry that we did it. This includes making a heartfelt apology.
- We feel and show compassion for how the other person has been hurt by our actions.

* We make amends for our wrongdoing. This is the equivalent of atonement, making up, in whatever way possible, for the imbalance we have caused.
* We make a commitment not to repeat it.

When someone refuses to respond positively and appreciatively to our repentance, we can feel compassion for his or her inability to let go. At the same time, we do not have to keep feeling guilty for our offensive behavior. We have done what we could do to right the wrong. Now it is up to the other person to follow suit and let any rancor go. If this does not happen it is not our fault; it is the choice of the offended person to remain a victim. An offended person who has psychological and spiritual health will be touched by our repentance and be willing to forgive rather than hold a grudge, give us the silent treatment, or worst of all, retaliate.

— ☙ —

Who by repentance is not satisfied
Is nor of heaven nor earth, for these are pleased.
By penitence the Eternal's wrath's appeased. (*Two Gentlemen of Verona*, Act V, Scene 4)

Both heaven and earth let go of anger when they see repentance. If we do not do the same, we lose our connection to the universe. After all, God himself lets go of the need to punish when people repent.

Sir, you have done enough, and have performed
A saint-like sorrow: no fault could you make,
Which you have not redeem'd; indeed, paid down
More penitence than done trespass: at the last,
Do as the heavens have done, forget your evil;
With them forgive yourself. (*The Winter's Tale*, Act V, Scene 1)

Making Amends

Sir, you have repented sufficiently. You have shown the sorrow and piety of a saint. You have made up for every mistake and have done more penance than was necessary. At last, forgive yourself for your sins as heaven has forgiven them.

Since when I have been debtor to you for courtesies,
which I will be ever to pay and yet pay still. (*Cymbeline*, Act I,
    Scene 4)

I am indebted to you for your goodness and am returning the thanks I owe you again and again.

...life is alter'd now:
I have done penance for contemning Love,
Whose high imperious thoughts have punish'd me
With bitter fasts, with penitential groans,
With nightly tears and daily heart-sore sighs;
For in revenge of my contempt of love,
Love hath chased sleep from my enthralled eyes
And made them watchers of mine own heart's sorrow.
    (*Two Gentlemen of Verona*, Act II, Scene 4)

I have experienced a spiritual change in my life. I have done penance for acting in an unloving way. I have been punished by my own pride, by my ongoing sorrow, and by sleeplessness, too.

Pray thee, peace. Pay her the debt you owe her, unpay the
    villainy you have done with her; the one you may do with
    sterling money, and the other with current repentance.
    (*Henry IV, Part Two*, Act II, Scene 1)

Show that you are sorry for treating her so unkindly both by paying the money you owe her and by repentance for your actions.

SPIRITUAL PRACTICES

Nature craves
All dues be render'd to their owners. (*Troilus and Cressida*, Act II,
Scene 2)

It is part of the very nature of things that we make amends and act
with fairness. (This fits with the ancient Latin saying, "Res clamat
domino," "A possession cries out for its owner.")

Pardon me, Edward, I will make amends:
And, Richard, do not frown upon my faults,
For I will henceforth be no more unconstant. (*Henry VI, Part*
Three, Act V, Scene 1)

I will make amends and do now ask forgiveness as I promise to act
with constancy in the future.

I desire you in friendship, and I will one way or other make you
amends. (*The Merry Wives of Windsor*, Act III, Scene 1)

I want your friendship and will find a way to make my amends to you.

Gentles, do not reprehend:
If you pardon, we will mend:
And, as I am an honest Puck,
If we have unearned luck
Now to 'scape the serpent's tongue,
We will make amends ere long.... (*A Midsummer's Night's Dream*,
Act V, Scene 1)

Gentle folk, do not hold anything against us. If you pardon us for
our faults, we will certainly make amends and soon too.

— ℮ℓ℮ —

Making Amends

A troubling obstacle to letting go of guilt is regret. The origin of the word *regret* is from an old Germanic word meaning "weep." Adding "re" makes it refer to intense repeated weeping. We keep crying over spilt milk. When we are obsessed with regret, we are spinning our wheels and going nowhere. It does not lead to processing an experience and resolving it. Grief is the healthy alternative to regret. When we fully mourn a distressing misbehavior or wrongdoing, we process and resolve it. Grief eventually lets us go so we can proceed on our journey.

When we have offended someone, we can practice using the steps in the introduction to this chapter: confession, contrition, compassion, amends, and commitment. These five steps show our willingness both to repent the past and heal the future. Before we were offenders; now we are penitents. If we still have regrets about past offenses against others, we can benefit from the following spiritual practice. It is a deeply humble affirmation based on the Mahayana Buddhist Full Moon Ritual:

All my ancient and twisted karma
from beginningless greed, hate, and ignorance
—born of body, speech, and mind—
I now fully avow, repent, and won't repeat.
By a wonderful grace
I am converted to Buddha's way,
the path of integrity and loving-kindness
and a refuge from every fear.
I bow in thanks to my spiritual allies.

23

Peacemaking within and around Us

A calling to all humans is peacemaking. We support political programs that attempt to bring peace to the world around us. We are committed to the path of nonviolence both in our personal life and in the wider world.

We look for ways to mend divisions and encourage our families and friends to stay in harmony and resolve differences. We follow the advice of Fr. Zossima in *The Brothers Karamazov* by Fyodor Dostoyevsky: "One wonders whether one should use force or gentle love. *Always choose gentle love.* If you resolve on that once and for all, you may subdue the whole world. Gentle love is marvelously strong, the strongest of all things. There is nothing else like it."

In Buddhism, there are four qualities of the enlightened mind: loving-kindness, compassion, joy at the success of others, and equanimity. Our practice is to apply these as ways of fostering peace. We show them not only to our near and dear but to all beings:

- We act with tender loving-kindness.
- We feel and show compassion.
- We are pleased when others find happiness. We are not envious of them; we are glad they have found success and tell them so.
- We cultivate equanimity that happens in us because of the first three practices. Equanimity is composure in distress, the capacity to roll with the punches in life, to remain stable through thick and thin. We maintain our stability when things fall apart.

All four of these engender peace in us and others: Loving-kindness and compassion foster an attitude of caring. Joy at the good fortune of others creates closeness, companionship, and strong connection. Equanimity leads to a serene handling of conflict and stress. Caring, compassion, connection, and stability mean no more war in relationships or on world stages.

— ☽ —

Now in peace my soul shall part to heaven,
Since I have set my friends at peace on earth. (*Richard III*, Act II,
    Scene 1)

I am ready to leave this world serenely as I see that I have helped those whom I love find peace.

How comes this gentle concord in the world
That hatred is so far from jealousy
To sleep by hate and fear no enemy? (A *Midsummer Night's
    Dream*, Act IV, Scene 1)

What a gift! There can be harmony between rivals when they are no longer jealous of one another.

133

SPIRITUAL PRACTICES

The fingers of the powers above do tune
The harmony of this peace. (*Cymbeline*, Act V, Scene 5)

We have divine approbation in finding peace.

The time of universal peace is near. (*Antony and Cleopatra*, Act
   IV, Scene 6)

We can trust the possibility of peace on earth.

An hour of quiet shortly shall we see;
Till then, in patience our proceeding be. (*Hamlet*, Act V, Scene 1)

Peace is very close. Till then, let's be patient.

At last, though long, our jarring notes agree:
And time it is, when raging war is done,
To smile at escapes and perils overblown. (*The Taming of the
   Shrew*, Act V, Scene 2)

*The time has finally come for an end to conflicts, when we can smile
at how we escaped from dangers.*

— ☙ —

Conflicts arise in any relationships, both at home and between
nations. Our calling is to mend not feud. We do this by commit-
ting ourselves to a practice of addressing, processing, and resolving conflicts that arise among us. To address is to name the issue
and to admit our part in it. To process is to share our feelings
about what has happened and to open ourselves to the feelings
of the other.

Once we have addressed and processed a concern in these
ways, we are more likely to find a solution. This can come in the
form of reconciling ourselves to one another, forgiving, and let-

ting go, our best pathways to peace. It can also take the form of an agreement to do things more skillfully and respectfully in the future. Peace is always possible when we believe it is. Our spiritual practices turn our beliefs into convictions and commitments that foster nonviolent solutions. This is how peace among individuals can result from conflicts—a spiritual irony.

World peace takes political change. It happens when nations forsake war as a solution to international conflicts. Instead, they keep looking for diplomatic solutions. On our part, we elect officials who are committed to this survival-based venture. We join with those who believe in the success of nonviolence. We join with those who protest war and injustice nonviolently. We support arms reduction rather than stand by while nuclear weapons keep proliferating. Most of all, we act with loving-kindness in all our personal dealings since that is where peace begins.

24

Gratitude for Graces

Grace is described in religious terms as a gift freely given by God that equips us to live God's life in the world. It also expands and boosts, and even creates a courage that is invincible and a love that is unconditional and universal. We receive graces not because of our merits or our accomplishments. They are freely given irrespective of our practices. All we need to do is be open to them.

In nonreligious terms, grace is the gift dimension of life. It is that extra assistance we need, that awakening that we know we did not cause. Something kicks in that expands the range of our efforts but is not the result of them. Something takes shape in us that readies us for a challenge we did not necessarily feel capable of facing. Suddenly or gradually, things happen that move us on our journey, without our having to be at the helm. Synchronicity is a major example of grace.

Our response to grace is gratitude. This includes thanks for synchronicities—how coincidences, circumstances, and events line up to help us grow. We show thanks to individuals who are kind to us without our having requested it. We adopt an attitude of gratitude toward the universe, God, or higher power, for all the benefits that come to us unbidden, minutely or abundantly.

Furthermore, since everything that happens to us provides us an opportunity for spiritual practice, everything that happens is a grace and calls for gratitude. Since all that happens can help us evolve into full humanness, we might say we always have reasons to be thankful.

We may also be conduits of grace to others. When others thank us, we let in their appreciation with an appreciation of our own toward them. When others do not thank us, we are sorry they have missed such a spiritual opportunity as gratitude. We do not hold resentment toward them. We continue to show them loving-kindness, our central practice of grace.

— ॐ —

[In] every wink of an eye some new grace will be born....
   (*The Winter's Tale*, Act V, Scene 2)

Graces keep coming to us in many simple ways.

It is a surplus of your grace. (*The Winter's Tale*, Act V, Scene 3)

What you give me comes from your virtuous generosity.

Convert his gyves to graces. (*Hamlet*, Act IV, Scene 7)

Turn his fetters into gifts.

Praised be God, and not our strength, for it! (*Henry V*, Act IV, Scene 7)

French soldier Mountjoy tells Henry that the English won the battle, and he acknowledges that it happened by divine grace rather than human will.

SPIRITUAL PRACTICES

God shall be my hope,
My stay, my guide, and lantern to my feet. (*Henry VI, Part Two,*
Act II, Scene 3)

I rely on a higher power for stability, guidance, and light on my path.

Love give me strength! and strength shall help afford. (*Romeo
and Juliet,* Act IV, Scene 1)

Love, give me the strength that will then help me.

Divinest patroness, and midwife gentle
To those that cry by night, convey thy deity
Aboard our dancing boat... (*Pericles,* Act III, Scene 1)

Divine Feminine, stabilize me on this shaky voyage of life.

Thou hast been
As one, in suffering all, that suffers nothing,
A man that fortune's buffets and rewards
Hast taken with equal thanks. (*Hamlet,* Act III, Scene 2)

*You are admirable when you accept the good with the bad and even
have gratitude for anything life hands you.*

Let us be thankful
For that which is. (*The Two Noble Kinsmen,* Act V, Scene 4)

We can be thankful for what is as it is.

O Lord, that lends me life,
Lend me a heart replete with thankfulness! (*Henry VI, Part Two,*
Act I, Scene 1)

I ask the higher power that gave me life to fill my heart with gratitude.

— ৯৪ —

The givens of life are the events over which we have no control, "the things we cannot change." An unconditional yes to them is our spiritual practice. We soon see that they are not burdens or penalties. They are the necessary ingredients for humans to have character, depth, and compassion. Likewise, our yes to the givens of life, no matter how trying they may be, is a direct path to inner peace. Our response is gratitude.

We are thankful for the way things are when we open to five main givens of life:

- *Everything changes and ends.* This means loss and consequent grief. Our gratitude is based on how we are deepening ourselves by grieving and letting go. Our gratitude opens us to what comes next in our life.
- *Things don't always go according to plan.* Our gratitude is for the new plans the universe makes for us, so challenging, so growth-inducing, so surprising. Our plans fall through, and thereby, we can glimpse a whole new range of possibilities.
- *Pain is part of life.* We are thankful for how we find healing in ourselves and in supportive others. We are thankful for the grace to feel compassion for those who suffer.
- *Life is not always fair.* We are grateful that we are committed to being fair no matter how others behave toward us. Our commitment is not simply a decision we have made. Our continued commitment is the results of the grace given to us.
- *People are not loyal or loving all the time.* We appreciate those who love us; we appreciate ourselves for our own loyalty and love toward others. We are thankful for the grace-capacity to go on loving even when others do not act lovingly toward us.

25

Prayer

Prayer is how we commune with God—the bigger-than-ego life within and around us. Prayer is contact with the divine essence within and beyond us. A prayerful response to what happens is staying present in it with love and integrity, open to its quiet or loud calling. Prayer is, then, an act of listening more than speaking. We mature spiritually when we trust that whatever happens to us is an opportunity for communion with the divine. Prayer is an opening to that grace.

The two best prayers are stated by the former and second Secretary-General of the United Nations, Dag Hammarskjold: "For all that has been: thanks. For all that will be: yes." Prayer is saying yes to what has happened. Yes to what has or is unfolding in our life is also expressed as "Thy will be done." Gratitude follows because we realize that everything that may happen next will be an opportunity to find divine love in ourselves and in the events of our lives. Then, we no longer pray that something starts or stops. We become open to what is starting and welcome it. We accept that something is ending and let it go.

As our prayer life of "yes" and "thanks" develops, we become more comfortable with challenges and more able to handle their wallop. That is the essence of prayer. St. Teresa of Avila wrote: "When we accept what happens to us and make the best of it, we are praising God." As this attitude pervades our day, we are, in effect, practicing what St. Luke recommends that we pray always (see Luke 21:36).

Any healthy experience, feeling, or spiritual practice can be a form of prayer. For example, we can connect prayer to what we discussed about the first given of life, that there will always be changes, losses, and endings. In a healthy response, we are accepting what we can't change *while* grieving it. This is how grief becomes a form of prayer; it is an acceptance of what is, that is, a surrender to a divine calling. In Shakespeare, we recall these lines: "The weight of this sad time we must obey [accept] / Speak what we feel [grieve], not what we ought to say [I accept what I can't change]." (*King Lear*, Act V, Scene 3)

— ﷺ —

Now, God be praised, that to believing souls
Gives light in darkness, comfort in despair. (*Henry VI, Part Two*,
    Act II, Scene 1)

When we have faith, our prayer leads to light and comfort.

Fair encounter
Of two most rare affections! Heavens rain grace
On that which breeds between them! (*The Tempest*, Act III,
    Scene 1)

May heaven bless the union of true lovers.

Now I am past all comforts here, but prayers. (*Henry VIII*,
    Act IV, Scene 2)

Sometimes, the only comfort we have left to us is prayer.

SPIRITUAL PRACTICES

We, ignorant of ourselves,
Beg often our own harms, which the wise powers
Deny us for our good; so find we profit
By losing of our prayers. (*Antony and Cleopatra*, Act II, Scene 1)

*Sometimes, we pray for something that is not in our best interests, so
it is our good fortune when such a prayer is not answered.*

If you bethink yourself of any crime
Unreconciled as yet to heaven and grace,
Solicit for it straight. (*Othello*, Act V, Scene 2)

Prayer includes asking forgiveness for our misdeeds.

My words fly up, my thoughts remain below:
Words without thoughts never to heaven go. (*Hamlet*, Act III,
    Scene 1)

Prayer requires a consonance of thought and words to be effective.

...we do pray for mercy;
And that same prayer doth teach us all to render
The deeds of mercy. (*The Merchant of Venice*, Act IV, Scene 1)

*The mercy for which we pray to God is also the mercy that we are
to show to others.*

...watch to-night, pray to-morrow.
Gallants, lads, boys, hearts of gold, all the titles
of good fellowship come to you! (*Henry IV, Part One*, Act II,
    Scene 4)

May our prayer lead to noble fellowship.

The above quotations show us some essential qualities of prayer:

- Our faith in prayer is really trust that light will always come through no matter how dark the world around us may be or become. There will always be comfort no matter how desperate the circumstances. Sometimes, prayer itself is the comfort. Likewise, our prayerful attitude gives us access to hope. It can stabilize us when things are falling apart—even when we are falling apart.
- Since we don't fully know ourselves or our needs, prayer can't be about getting a rescuer-God to do what we decide is best for us. However, what turns out to be best for us becomes clear precisely in how our prayers are answered.
- Prayer is also a way of repenting for our offenses and finding forgiveness. Thus, prayer is a promise that reconciliation is always possible. Of course, it will be important to align our hearts and our words along the way.
- Our prayerful attitude makes us more likely to love others, to find communion with and be compassionate toward them. This is because listening to the divine voice—true prayer—establishes and sustains connection with all beings. Indeed, deepest experience of prayer is a mystical attunement to the entire universe.

Finally, since poetry takes us to the transcendent, it is itself a form of prayer, contact with the divine life in all that is. Shakespeare shows us that a poet sees beyond what is and reveals what can be, beyond how we act to what we are, beyond time into eternity. In that sense, poetry is a voyage into the spiritual world, and a poet can pilot us to it:

SPIRITUAL PRACTICES

The poet's eye, in fine frenzy rolling,
Doth glance from heaven to earth, from earth to heaven;
And as imagination bodies forth
The forms of things unknown, the poet's pen
Turns them to shapes and gives to airy nothing
A local habitation and a name. (*A Midsummer's Night's Dream*,
   Act V, Scene 1)

— ℰ —

I say Yes to everything that happens to me today
as an opportunity
to give or receive love and to free myself from fear.
I am thankful for the enduring capacity to love
that has come to me from the Sacred Heart of the universe.
May everything that happens to me today
open my heart more and more.
May all that I think, say, feel, do, and am express loving-kindness
toward myself, those close to me, and all beings.

Epilogue

~

The primary way to discover depth and meaning in Shakespeare is by watching—and enjoying—his plays. This also becomes a most effective way to enter the human story in all its variety. We find out how humans feel, how humans behave, how humans become humane or the opposite. We are those humans as the distance between stage and seat disappears.

This book has opened and explored many topics, but there is no substitute for being in an audience at the plays. Here is an example of how that experience made a powerful impact on me. I was in a theater watching the 1971 version of *King Lear* with Lear played by Paul Scofield. This play is a story of unrelieved grief and irreparable regret. Unexplainably, more than ever in my life, I became thoroughly absorbed in, even possessed by, the drama as it kept unfolding. I could tell that my whole being was wrenched in attentiveness to the unrelieved tragedy. At the same time, my body was in a heightened state of stress. When Lear recited what I consider the most powerful line in all of Shakespeare's works, I began to weep uncontrollably. It is five repetitions of the word *never* as Lear confronts the death of his only loving and only beloved daughter, Cordelia: "Never, never, never, never, never."

With each "never" I felt a deeper piercing of a part of my soul that I never knew was in me. Each "never" was a gong from the belfry of the last remaining cathedral on a devastated earth tolling the expiration of all any human could hold dear. And I was that human. It was an unforgettable and infallible example of the power of Shakespeare. I found out more trenchantly than ever what can happen when I let myself participate fully in the experience of his characters.

Nelson Mandela, son of a Xhosa chief, was born and grew up in Transkei, six thousand miles from Britain. English was not his mother tongue, yet he once said, "Shakespeare always seems to have something to say to us." In Mandela's words, the "never" in *King Lear* has turned into his "always" in our mutual experience of humanness.

O, wonder!
How many goodly creatures are there here!
How beauteous mankind is! O brave new world,
That has such people in it! (*The Tempest*, Act V, Scene 1)

Appendix

For sheer amusement, I share my own attempt at a poem in the style of Shakespeare. Here is my version of Glinda's final speech to Dorothy from the film, *The Wizard of Oz*, when she has lost hope about ever getting back home to Kansas:

Be not afear'd, thou art not stranded here,
Thou joy of Kansas, gift of Jove to us,
Whom timely cyclone pitched to our domain,
By choice or chance, to win us all from woe.
Thou art the sweet reluctant nemesis
My ill-starred sister faced in fiendish wrath
When, visage green with envious spite, she groaned
To see her slippers fit so firm on thee.
Hail, valiant pilgrim, rubied in thy worth,
Who with the shield Athena Perseus gave
Didst slay Medusa but wast not slain too.
Hail, grounding force of sky-borne monkeys who
Were once so cruel, now happy to be kind.
Thou didst recall the troops, not muster them
As tim'rous king, of crown unsure, will send
To far-off lands our bravest corps, his throne
To verify. Beholden denizens
Of newly-ransomed Oz give tender thanks

TO THINE OWN SELF BE TRUE

To thee and to thy scarred but rugged friends:
A scarecrow stuffed secure with caring wit,
A tin man blessed with heart and tears alike,
A lion bold to growl and stand up tall,
And most of all, thy winsome daring dog,
The little pilot of this whole crusade,
The selfless, loving, loyal boast and best,
Who drew the drape that hid the wizard's feint.
O'er all of you we pass our wand with grace,
And, as thou exit from this globe, we grieve
Like lonesome cygnets, who, with sighful peeps,
Will hark the dirge their mother croons at last
And nestle, rueful, nigh her downy breast,
Perchance her brooding feathers one more time
Might lull them as in bygone warm white days.
So cling we to our moment final here
With thee—and yet we have to let thee go
That thou mightst haste thy way to sepia lands
And sing again thy rainbow bluebird song,
The Orphic hymn that wakes dun Hades' drowse
And ushers souls to glimpse the prairie's glow.
No need for zeppelin hurled by fickle wind,
No need for bungling wizardry at helm,
No need for sulfur, magic, or for gong,
Great heart, you've had the power all along!

Paulist Books by David Richo

How to Be an Adult: A Handbook on Psychological and Spiritual Integration (1991)

Happy, mature people have learned the knack of being generous with their sympathies while still taking care of themselves. We can all evolve from the neurotic ego through a healthy ego to the spiritual Self. We can deal with fear, anger, and guilt. We can be assertive, have boundaries, and build intimacy.

When Love Meets Fear: Becoming Defense-less and Resource-full (1997; rev. ed., 2022)

Our lively energy is inhibited by fear, and we are so often needlessly on the defensive. We consider the origins and healings of our fears of closeness, commitment, aloneness, assertiveness, and panic attacks. We can free ourselves from the grip of fear so that it no longer stops or drives us.

The Sacred Heart of the World: Restoring Mystical Devotion to Our Spiritual Life (2007)

We explore the symbolism of the heart in world religious traditions, and then trace the historical thread of Christian devotion to the Sacred Heart of Jesus into modern times. We focus on the philosophy and theology of Teilhard de Chardin and Karl Rahner to design a new sense of what devotion can be.

How to Be an Adult in Faith and Spirituality (2011)

We explore and compare religion and spirituality with an emphasis on how they can both become rich resources for personal growth. We increase our understanding of God, faith, and life's plaguing questions in the light of mysticism, depth psychology, and our new appreciation of evolutionary cosmology.

When Catholic Means Cosmic: Opening to a Big-Hearted Faith (2015)

When Catholic has cosmic dimensions, we and our religion expand. In other words, we update our beliefs in accord with the best advances in psychology and science. We maintain and appreciate the riches of our religion while being contemporary. People of all traditions will find this book helpful since we explore how religion and spirituality can be integrated.

When Mary Becomes Cosmic: A Jungian and Mystical Path to the Divine Feminine (2016)

Our vision of Mary can become cosmic in scope. The Jungian archetype of the divine feminine as personified by Mary is built into the design of every human psyche. Her ancient titles reflect the marvelous qualities of our own essential Self and Mother Earth. Every religious truth and image are a metaphor for us and the world.

Everything Ablaze: Meditating on the Mystical Vision of Teilhard de Chardin (2017)

Contemporary interest in the work of Teilhard de Chardin manifests the evolutionary mysticism he taught and forecast and that we can apply to our daily life. This is conscious evolution, a presence in the world as members of Christ's body. It is then that we co-create the future of justice, peace, and love that Christ came to proclaim, spread and be.

Other Books by David Richo

Shadow Dance: Liberating the Power and Creativity of Your Dark Side (Shambhala, 1999)

How To Be an Adult in Relationships: The Five Keys to Mindful Loving (Shambhala, 2002; rev. ed., 2021)

The Five Things We Cannot Change…: And the Happiness We Find by Embracing Them (Shambhala, 2005)

The Power of Coincidence: How Life Shows Us What We Need to Know (Shambhala, 2007)

When the Past Is Present: Healing the Emotional Wounds That Sabotage Our Relationships (Shambhala, 2008)

Being True to Life: Poetic Paths to Personal Growth (Shambhala, 2009)

Daring to Trust: Opening Ourselves to Real Love and Intimacy (Shambhala, 2010)

Coming Home to Who You Are: Discovering Your Natural Capacity for Love, Integrity, and Compassion (Shambhala, 2011)

How To Be an Adult in Love: Letting Love in Safely and Showing It Recklessly (Shambhala, 2013)

The Power of Grace: Recognizing Unexpected Gifts on Our Path (Shambhala, 2014)

You Are Not What You Think: The Egoless Path to Self-Esteem and Generous Love (Shambhala, 2015)

TO THINE OWN SELF BE TRUE

The Five Longings: What We've Always Wanted and Already Have (Shambhala, 2017)

Five True Things: A Little Guide to Embracing Life's Big Challenges (Shambhala, 2019)

Triggers: How We Can Stop Reacting and Start Healing (Shambhala, 2019)

Wholeness and Holiness: How to Be Sane, Spiritual, and Saintly (Orbis Books, 2020)

Ready: How to Know When to Go and When to Stay (Shambhala, 2022)

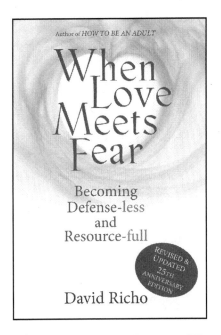

Author of *HOW TO BE AN ADULT*

When Love Meets Fear

Becoming
Defense-less
and
Resource-full

REVISED & UPDATED 25TH ANNIVERSARY EDITION

David Richo

When Love Meets Fear

Becoming Defense-less
and Resource-full

David Richo

This book is for people who want to let go of unreasonable fear or act more creatively in the face of reasonable fear. It explores the roots of fear—the fear of change, of self-disclosure, of giving and receiving, of being alone. Beneath all of these is the greatest fear of all: the fear of loving and being loved. This new edition has been greatly updated and expanded to include more contemporary developments in psychology and current events. Every chapter of the book has been rewritten and revised with a new audience in mind. Some new sections have been added and existing sections revised.

5573-6 • $29.95